The Poetry of Alexander Pope

David Fairer, M.A., D.Phil. (Oxon.) read English at Trinity College, Oxford, and was appointed Junior Research Fellow at The Queen's College, Oxford, 1971–5, and lecturer in English at Christ Church, 1975–6. He is now lecturer in English at the University of Leeds. Dr Fairer is the author of *Pope's Imagination* (Manchester University Press, 1984) and has published many articles and reviews on the eighteenth century. He is currently writing a book on the symbolic representation of women in poetry and drama.

Penguin Critical Studies
Advisory Editors:
Stephen Coote and Bryan Loughrey

The Poetry of Alexander Pope

David Fairer

Penguin Books

PENGUIN BOOKS

Published by the Penguin Group
27 Wrights Lane, London W8 5TZ, England
Viking Penguin Inc., 40 West 23rd Street, New York, New York 10010, USA
Penguin Books Australia Ltd, Ringwood, Victoria, Australia
Penguin Books Canada Ltd, 2801 John Street, Markham, Ontario, Canada L3R 1B4
Penguin Books (NZ) Ltd, 182–190 Wairau Road, Auckland 10, New Zealand

Penguin Books Ltd, Registered Offices: Harmondsworth, Middlesex, England

First published 1989
10 9 8 7 6 5 4 3 2 1

Copyright © David Fairer, 1989
All rights reserved

Made and printed in Great Britain by
Richard Clay Ltd, Bungay, Suffolk
Filmset in Monophoto Times

For Richard, Christine, Kristin,
Eric and Urmi

Contents

	Introduction	ix
	Pope's Life: A Brief Chronology	xi
1.	Life and Art	1
2.	The Techniques of Pope's Verse	15
3.	*An Essay on Criticism*	30
	(i) The Critical Context	30
	(ii) The Poem	34
4.	*Windsor Forest*	41
5.	*The Rape of the Lock*	50
	(i) The Plot of the Poem	51
	(ii) Mock-heroic	55
	(iii) Belinda and the Sylphs	62
6.	*Elegy to the Memory of an Unfortunate Lady*	66
7.	*Eloisa to Abelard*	70
8.	*An Essay on Man*	75
	(i) The Intellectual Context	76
	(ii) The Poem	80
9.	*Epistle to Burlington*	91
10.	*Epistle to a Lady*	101
11.	*Epistle to Arbuthnot*	110
12.	Pope and Horace	119
13.	*The Dunciad*	135
	(i) The Growth of the Poem	135
	(ii) A Commentary on the 1743 *Dunciad*	138
	(iii) The Nature of Dulness	150
	List of Further Reading	159

Introduction

This book is designed as an introduction to the poetry of Alexander Pope for students of all ages, but especially for those who are studying eighteenth-century verse for the first time. The excitements of reading Pope last a lifetime, and yet the first encounter can often be a cautious and puzzling one. We are greeted by beautifully shaped rhyming couplets, by verse that seems artificial, contained and regular. We may have been told that the Eighteenth Century was an Age of Reason, Correctness and Decorum (all with capital letters), and certainly this poetry seems to lack the 'spontaneous overflow' we expect from the later Romantic verse of Wordsworth and others.

How wrong we would be to stop there. Pope's poems have more vigour, vision and intensity than much romantic or modern verse, and the secret is his uncanny ability to compress and direct the power of words. The heroic couplet (which he uses in all these poems) does not restrict him – it increases the vitality of his language by making every word count. Nor does it restrict his scale – he can move within a single line (as he does in *The Rape of the Lock*) from the trinkets on Belinda's dressing-table to the universe itself, from the 'cosmetic' to the 'cosmic'. His poems are forever reaching outwards to explore ideas about mankind and the world, and at another moment they take us into the individual unconscious.

Pope's verse is peopled by an extraordinary collection of personalities: eccentrics, lunatics, suicides, pompous asses, saints and devils. The unlucky objects of his satire are not attacked, they are exposed (a different art altogether), their inner weakness, rottenness or stupidity mercilessly laid bare. Yet in many cases Pope uncovers the tragedy as well as the farce, and sometimes his imagination engages itself so fully that the result is a kind of appalled sympathy.

Pope is not a satirist, but a poet who writes satire. And the distinction is important. Unlike his close friend Swift, whose whole life seems to have consisted of a satirical outlook and the putting-on of a series of satirical disguises, Pope was very much the general man of letters (as editor, translator, formal letter-writer), and some of his finest poems are not satires: *An Essay on Man, An Essay on Criticism, Windsor Forest, Eloisa to Abelard* and many other shorter pieces. 'Satirical' in any case can be a dangerously limiting word. It narrows our thoughts to the notion of *attack*, and we tend to ask questions such as 'What or whom is he attacking?', 'How does he go about it?', 'Do we think he succeeds?', 'Is he being fair?'. These questions end in a cul-de-sac. We have to realize that satirical poetry is forced to *create* what it attacks – there is not something already there (as there would be if we drew a moustache on the Mona Lisa). Pope brings into being the very world that disturbs and provokes him. The 'meaning' of the unforgettable 'Sporus'-passage from *Epistle to Arbuthnot*, for instance, does not lie in comparing Pope's 'portrait' with the real Lord Hervey; it lies rather in how Pope creates an ambiguous, disturbing figure who haunts our imaginations. Whether he is 'fair' to Hervey is a question belonging to history, not literature.

In this book I have not aimed to write a 'handbook' to Pope, but instead one which focuses on the act of reading his poems and on the difficulties and excitements this involves. For a poet as allusive as Pope it is necessary to have a certain amount of background information; a well-annotated edition is an enormous help, and in discussing individual works I have tried to place each one in its context, against a setting of ideas or facts which become part of the poem's meaning. At appropriate moments I have attempted to clarify the complexities surrounding certain vital words (such as *wit, sense, nature* etc.) which do a great deal of work in Pope's poetry.

Of course, some poems are now more accessible than others. *The Rape of the Lock* and *Epistle to Arbuthnot* regularly occur on A-level syllabuses, but *An Essay on Man* and the several *Imitations of Horace* are less easy to appreciate nowadays. In Chapters 8 and 12, therefore, the material is necessarily a little more complex, but the rewards of understanding these poems are great, and they can tell us a lot about Pope as a man and an artist.

Lack of space prevents me from including a discussion of Pope's translations of Homer's epics, the *Iliad* and the *Odyssey*. In his own day Pope's fame partly rested on these works, and certainly they make a powerful artistic impact – but only if read at length. Some of the poems' formal speeches have a stiffness and grandiloquence which have not worn well, but the descriptive passages are often richly textured, intense and moving, and over a prolonged reading the cumulative effect can be very powerful indeed.

Pope's life and art are intimately connected, and so I have included a first chapter which attempts to reveal some links, while providing an overview of his career and friendships. The brief chronology of his life will I hope serve as a useful reference-point.

Reading and teaching Pope remains a fresh adventure each time. This book is dedicated to a group with whom exploring him was a special delight.

Pope's Life: A Brief Chronology

1688 (21 May)	Alexander Pope born in London.
c.1700	The Pope family moves to Binfield in Windsor Forest.
1709 (May)	The *Pastorals*.
1711 (May)	*An Essay on Criticism*.
1712 (May)	*The Rape of the Lock* (two-canto version).
1713 (March)	*Windsor Forest*.
1714	The Scriblerus Club meets regularly.
(March)	*The Rape of the Lock* (five-canto version).
(Aug)	Queen Anne dies.
1715 (Mar)	Lord Bolingbroke flees to France.
(June)	Homer's *Iliad*, Volume I. Pope completes this six-volume translation in 1720.
1716 (Apr)	The Pope family settles at Chiswick.
1717 (June)	Pope's *Works* (a collected volume which includes *Elegy to the Memory of an Unfortunate Lady* and *Eloisa to Abelard*).
1719	Pope moves to Twickenham.
1725	Bolingbroke returns to England.
(March)	Pope's edition of Shakespeare.
(April)	Homer's *Odyssey*, Volumes I–III. This five-volume translation is completed in 1726.
1726 (Mar–Aug)	Swift in England to arrange the publication of *Gulliver's Travels*.
1728 (May)	*The Dunciad*, in three books.
1729 (April)	*The Dunciad Variorum*.
1731 (Dec)	*Epistle to Burlington*.
1732 (Dec)	John Gay dies.
1733 (Feb)	*Imitation of Horace* (Satire II.1, to Fortescue).
(Feb–May)	*An Essay on Man*, Epistles i–iii.
(Jun)	Pope's mother dies, aged 90.
1734 (Jan)	*An Essay on Man*, Epistle iv.
(Jul)	*Imitation of Horace* (Satire II.2, to Bethel).
(Dec)	*Sober Advice from Horace*.
1735 (Jan 2)	*Epistle to Dr Arbuthnot*.

Critical Studies: Poetry of Alexander Pope

(Jan 27)	Dr Arbuthnot dies.
(Feb)	*Epistle to a Lady.*
1738 (Mar)	*Imitation of Horace* (Epistle I.1, to Bolingbroke).
(May & Jul)	*Epilogue to the Satires*, Dialogues I and II.
1742 (Mar)	*The New Dunciad.*
1743 (Oct)	*The Dunciad*, in four books.
1744 (May 30)	Pope dies.

1. Life and Art

As a young man Pope must have felt himself designed to be an outsider. Being both a Roman Catholic and a cripple threatened to restrict him professionally, socially, emotionally and physically. But the old idea of Pope as the twisted satirist taking revenge on a world that had damaged him is, thankfully, exploded. We can now see that his life and art actually gain power from restriction. Pope knows that energies are more powerful when they are contained and harnessed, and that a negative 'repression' can turn into a more positive 'compression'. Instead of being randomly dispersed the energy can be concentrated and effectively put to work. This is evident in his use of the apparently restrictive heroic couplet and in the way some of his best poems reveal a fascination with ideas of containment and release. The twin restrictions under which he lived only encouraged him to find ways of turning to positive use the pressures they placed on him.

The year of Pope's birth into a Roman Catholic family was a momentous one in British history. In 1688 the Catholic king, James II, fled to France and his son-in-law, the Protestant Prince William of Orange, was invited from Holland to take the throne as William III. This bloodless revolution was of permanent significance for England's Catholics. They began to suffer a series of repressive measures, and by the time of Pope's adolescence Catholics were viciously discriminated against in many aspects of life. If Pope wished to, he could not vote, attend university, enter politics or the professions, or become a schoolmaster; he could not possess a horse of over £5 in value; he could not own a house within ten miles of London; nor could he inherit property. Also, any prominent Catholic was always in danger of being labelled a traitor and 'Jacobite' (someone who sought to restore the throne to the exiled 'Old Pretender', son of James II). This became a routine accusatic﹀ against Pope and shows how religion and politics were two faces of a single coin.

Yet, however much his friends in later life persuaded him to renounce his religion, he clung to his Roman Catholic faith. But even as he did so, he refused to think of himself as a member of a sect or an oppressed minority. On the contrary, his reaction was to assert that his principles were genuinely 'catholic' (or 'universal') ones:

I am a Catholick, in the strictest sense of the word ... the things I have always wished to see are not a Roman Catholick, or a French Catholick, or a Spanish Catholick, but a true Catholick: and not a King of Whigs, or a King of Tories, but a King of England.

(Pope to Atterbury, 20 November 1717)

Pope presents his private faith as a universal ideal. He throws the label *Catholick* back in the faces of those who would categorize and restrict him. In this way an intended negative is turned into a positive. Pope reverses the situation so that he occupies the centre and his enemies are dismissed as sectarian and unpatriotic. This tactic is typical of much of Pope's writing on politics, religion and morality.

Pope's physical handicap was a more tangible one. As a result of a tubercular infection which set in during his teens, he became in maturity a hunchbacked cripple no more than 4′ 6″ high. He never seemed free of the many ailments resulting from wasting bones and shortness of breath, and late in life he was a virtual invalid and had to be strapped into a stiff corset before he could stand. No wonder he spoke in *Epistle to Arbuthnot* of 'this long Disease, my Life' (132). But if his carcase (as he called it) was deformed, he was compensated with a spirited and sensitive face which he delighted to have painted and sculpted.

Though Pope felt his physical restrictions keenly, he also appreciated how his mind, by contrast, was free. Often in his letters we find him comparing the incapacities of his body with the power of his mind and the energy of his imagination:

Like a witch, whose Carcase lies motionless on the floor, while she keeps her airy Sabbaths, & enjoys a thousand Imaginary Entertainments abroad, in this world, & in others, I seem to sleep in the midst of the Hurry, even as you would swear a Top stands still, when tis in the Whirle of its giddy motion.

(to John Caryll Jr, 5 December 1712)

And in writing to his distant friends he tends to see his nature as a dual one: a crippled body enclosing a free and unbounded soul:

Were not my own Carcase (very little suited to my Soul) my worst Enemy, were it not for the *Body of this Death*, (as St Paul calls it) I would not be separated from you

(to Lord Orrery, 10 May 1736)

In such ways Pope fought against restriction. Attacked as a Roman Catholic and Jacobite, he turned the accusation round and projected himself as someone who clung to an older patriotic ideal. Attacked as a deformed cripple whose outward shape symbolized his twisted mind, Pope explored in his poetry how the inner life could transcend restriction and open itself out to wider experiences and universal values.

As we shall see, this becomes an important theme in *An Essay on Man* (where self-love expands into universal love), and it has a literary counterpart in Pope's discussion of the 'rules' of writing in *An Essay on Criticism* (where they are subordinated to the wider and more humane 'rules' of Nature). In *Windsor Forest* an enclosed place where ideals have been preserved is seen as opening out and spreading its principles across the world. In the *Imitations of Horace* a similar movement occurs when Pope (within the confines of classical imitation) projects his personal ideals as universal values. In some of his earlier poems figures like Eloisa, the Unfortunate Lady and Belinda are repressed by themselves or by others and seek different means of release. In the epistles *To Burlington*, *To a Lady*, and *To Arbuthnot* Pope turns his private friendships into public statements of principle. *The Dunciad* is of course the nightmare climax of these ideas, with its memorable picture of the goddess Dulness, the principle of repression itself, parading as a messiah of personal liberation.

Settled in the village of Binfield, within Windsor Forest, Pope seems to have been a precocious youth. He had been privately tutored, had attended a couple of Roman Catholic schools, and was already becoming proficient in the classical languages, turning his hand to translating Latin and Greek poetry and also to imitating older English writers such as Chaucer and Spenser – 'I lisp'd in Numbers', said Pope later in life (*Epistle to Arbuthnot*, 128). As a teenager he began to make valuable literary friendships with men much older than himself: Dr Samuel Garth, William Walsh and his forest neighbour Sir William Trumbull, all of whom Pope later celebrated for the encouragement and advice they had given him. His first published verses, the *Pastorals* (which appeared in a poetical miscellany in 1709), had been passed round them and bore the fruit of much helpful advice, particularly from Walsh. Pope knew that many great poets such as Virgil, Spenser and Milton had launched their poetic careers with pastorals, and these four elegant little pieces set in the different seasons of the year were intended to announce that a brilliant new talent was on the horizon.

The first three pastorals were dedicated to Trumbull, Garth, and William Wycherley (the famous comic dramatist of Charles II's time). This latter was perhaps the oddest and most influential of Pope's early relationships. Wycherley was in his late sixties and attempting to recapture his past success by publishing his verses. He asked his young friend to help him revise the poems, and from Pope's correspondence with him we can see how he painstakingly set about the task. Wycherley's outdated Restoration 'wit' (obviously a delight to the ladies of Charles II's court) was ruthlessly pruned. Under Pope's hand Wycherley's rakish gallantry became elegance, elaborate images and fanciful ideas were toned down and given shape, and in some cases the old man's poems became unrecognizable.

In some ways the fruit of Pope's friendship with Wycherley can be seen in *An Essay on Criticism* (1711), with its assertion of 'true Wit' as against the 'glaring Chaos' of false witticism. This ambitious verse-essay was a turning-point in Pope's career. *The Spectator* (edited by Joseph Addison) hailed it as a masterpiece. But the review which cut deepest was from the pen of John Dennis (the 'Appius' of lines 585–7). Dennis was an established and respected critic, but his furious pamphlet, *Reflections Critical and Satyrical, upon a late Rhapsody, call'd an Essay upon Criticism*, went beyond intellectual debate. He proceeded to revile Pope personally as 'a hunch-back'd Toad', sneered at his family and friends, and accused him of being a Jacobite. These were to become familiar lines of attack as Pope grew older, but it is ironic that the first vicious assault should have been triggered off by a poem which tries to project criticism as an enlightened and humane discipline.

The years 1710 to 1714 were exciting ones for Pope. He was a rising star in London's literary world and was forming lifelong friendships with men whose company was enormously stimulating to his own creativity. 'The Scriblerus Club' was the name given to the small group of friends (Pope himself, John Gay, Dr John Arbuthnot, Thomas Parnell and Jonathan Swift) who met regularly during this time, partly out of sheer pleasure at each other's company, but also to plan various satirical projects.

They were a sparkling mixture: Gay was full of boyish humour, a skilled parodist who later became the toast of London with his satiric musical *The Beggar's Opera* (1728); the jovial and absent-minded Arbuthnot was one of Queen Anne's physicians and author of a political satire, *The History of John Bull*; and Parnell, a promising Irish poet, was also something of a practical joker. But the man who had the most profound and lasting influence on Pope's work was that other Irishman, Jonathan Swift. Satire was in Swift's bones, and the wealth and range of his satirical writings is remarkable. He was a brilliant impersonator of voices and attitudes, a man who could expose nastiness, cruelty or folly by speaking its own language – to subtle and merciless effect. *Gulliver's Travels* (1726) is the most enduring of his works, but *A Tale of a Tub* and *A Modest Proposal* show other sides of his disturbing and complex personality. After 1714 until his death in 1745 Swift (now Dean of St Patrick's Cathedral, Dublin) was rarely in England, and so this important literary friendship often had to be confined to letters.

The literary pretext for the club's meetings was to compile *The Memoirs of Martinus Scriblerus*. These were planned as a satire on the misdirections and excesses of contemporary science, learning and culture. The fictional Scriblerus was presented as a pedant stuffed with flimsy and impractical knowledge, and all the club members contributed ideas. But it was Pope who eventually saw the project through and put the materials into shape. The *Memoirs* were published among his *Prose Works* in 1741. By that time, of course, the influence of Scriblerus had made itself felt in several satires of Gay, Swift and Pope, whose *Dunciad* (1728–43) is the most enduring monument to the club. It is significant that the poem's preface appears under the name of 'Martinus Scriblerus' and that some of the funniest mock-footnotes are attributed to him.

For a young man embarking on a literary career the question of money could not be ignored. It was possible to scrape a living by turning out pamphlets, articles, reports and reviews. There were always party newspapers willing to pay for satirical attacks on the opposition or for eloquent defences of government policy, and money was available from ministers or the nobility in response to a handsome dedication. Dr Johnson in the 1740s doggedly survived by journalistic hack-work until he made his name as an essayist and dictionary-writer; in contrast, Joseph Addison left Oxford after a successful university career and spent several years travelling round Europe on a government grant. He used the patronage-network well and by his mid-thirties was a literary patron himself, surrounded at Button's Coffee House by a group of young admirers (of whom Pope, for a time, was one).

Facing a choice between the independent road and the patronage road, Pope in 1713 took a momentous decision which made his name and allowed him to live without financial worries for the rest of his life. He embarked on a translation of Homer's *Iliad*, to be issued by subscription in six volumes, handsomely produced and with notes. This ambitious project was both a scholarly and poetic challenge, and it did not succeed without a fight. The first volume was published in June 1715, and just two days later a rival translation of Book One appeared, written by

Addison's protégé Thomas Tickell, and it was clear that the Whig 'little senate' at Button's (from whom Pope was becoming estranged) were out to discredit him. But Pope's translation won the battle, and by the time the final volumes were issued in 1720 it was already on the way to becoming a classic. After Addison's death in 1719 it was Pope who became the leading literary figure of the day.

In 1717, still in his twenties, Pope oversaw the publication of his *Works* (normally something to crown a literary career, rather than establish it). This handsome edition included new pieces such as *Eloisa to Abelard* and *Elegy to the Memory of an Unfortunate Lady* and an elegant preface in which Pope presented his works to the public with hesitant modesty, while at the same time consciously setting himself up for comparison with the ancient classical authors:

All that is left us is to recommend our productions by the imitation of the Ancients: and it will be found true, that in every age, the highest character for sense and learning has been obtain'd by those who have been most indebted to them. For to say truth, whatever is very good sense must have been common sense in all times; and what we call Learning, is but the knowledge of the sense of our predecessors.

The 1717 collected *Works* marks the end of Pope's early career as a poet. Not until 1728 does an original poem of any importance appear. These eleven years may seem a gap in Pope's creativity. In fact they were very busy ones. After the success of the *Iliad* Pope embarked on a companion translation of that other Homeric epic, the *Odyssey*, this time with the assistance of two friends, William Broome and Elijah Fenton (who translated half the poem between them, though under Pope's supervision). He was also working hard during these years on a six-volume edition of Shakespeare, which made its appearance in 1725.

This period of translating and editing was poetically productive in an indirect way since it focused Pope's attention on the two writers who were for him the great poets of human nature. '*Nature* and *Homer* were, he found, the *same*', Pope had written in line 135 of *An Essay on Criticism*, and in his preface to the edition of Shakespeare: 'he is not so much an Imitator, as an Instrument, of Nature'. Pope's years of detailed study therefore gave him insight into the work of two writers who spoke a universal language of human feeling, yet whose verse could hardly have been more different: the epic sweep and grandeur of Homer, and Shakespeare's dramatic mastery of tone and verbal subtlety. *The Dunciad* and *Epistle to a Lady* could not have been written without Pope's 'ten years to comment and translate' (*Dunciad*, iii, 332).

For Pope and his closest friends the years after 1714 were a time when the political sky was darkening. Before that date the members of the Scriblerus Club felt very much in the swim of politics and public affairs. From 1710 to 1714 Swift was the leading journalist of the Tory government and wrote powerful pamphlets in support of their negotiations to end the war with France. A welcome guest at their meetings was the Chief Minister, Robert Harley, later Earl of Oxford, who enjoyed exchanging state business for the informality of the club and became a friend of Pope's.

The composition of political parties during the eighteenth century is notoriously complex. Political allegiances tended to be far more fluid than they are today, and a political 'party' could form round an influential individual or a small group of likeminded people. The terms 'Tory' and 'Whig' should be confined to the larger and more open groupings according to general principle.

Some issues tended to polarize government and opposition, and in the later years of Queen Anne's reign (1702–14) the debate centred on the war with France. The Whig government before 1710 had supported the war and had lavishly rewarded the victorious general, the Duke of Marlborough. In 1710 a Tory ministry was formed, Marlborough was eventually dismissed, and the government was determined to bring the expensive war to an end. The Whigs (whose strength lay in London and the City) protested that the fruits of Marlborough's victories were being thrown away. The Tories,* however, with their bias towards the 'landed' country interest, wished to end the penal land tax that had supported the war (and which Catholics had to pay double). The long negotiations concluded in the Peace of Utrecht, celebrated in Pope's *Windsor Forest* (1713), a poem which shrewdly emphasizes the beneficial effects of the Tory Peace on trade and the expansion of British interest abroad.

The death of Queen Anne in 1714 marked a momentous change in the political world. The new King (the German-speaking Hanoverian, George I) sent for the Whigs and the pendulum swung away from Pope and his Tory friends. The England of the Stuarts became 'Georgian' England, and an attempt the following year to restore the Stuart pretender as James III ended humiliatingly when the first Jacobite Rising was suppressed. In the aftermath of the 1715 rebellion Harley was imprisoned in the Tower for two years waiting to be tried on a trumped-up

---

* There is no connection, incidentally, save name, with the modern 'Tory' party, which in many ways is closer to the principles and power-base of the eighteenth-century Whigs.

treason charge. English Catholics found themselves in an uncomfortable position, and the Whig government did all it could to identify and punish prominent Jacobites. Pope himself became involved, not just as a suspected Jacobite himself, but through his support of two very close friends, Bolingbroke and Atterbury.

Henry St John, Viscount Bolingbroke, had been a Tory Secretary of State, but in 1715 he fled to France where he became the leading 'minister' of the Pretender. In 1723 he was pardoned and returned to England, eventually settling on his farm near Uxbridge where he waited for the nation's call (which never came). Pope's admiration for Bolingbroke was boundless, and he took virtually every opportunity to acknowledge his friendship and celebrate Bolingbroke's virtues – even when it was dangerous to do so. Francis Atterbury, Bishop of Rochester and Dean of Westminster (and in effect the leader of the Jacobite activists) was another intimate friend, and Pope must have been profoundly shocked when in 1722 Atterbury was thrown into the Tower to await trial for treason. At the 'trial' before the House of Lords the following year Pope actually gave evidence, but the new chief minister, Robert Walpole, was implacable and nothing could prevent Atterbury's sentence of exile for life. Pope, however, risked prosecution by continuing to correspond with his friend.

Pope remained to the end devoted to these two supposed 'traitors', and his idealization of them was only enhanced by their exile. This tells us a lot about Pope's developing conviction that power and virtue are contradictory things, and his sense that true moral principles can only be cultivated at a remove from Court and Government. In the 1720s Pope was gaining an increasing reputation as an 'opposition' figure, as a man who refused to compromise with authority or accept government patronage (on which so many writers depended). Pope himself was proud of this independence, and in a letter to the Secretary of State, Lord Carteret, he refused to renounce Atterbury:

I love my Country, better than any Personal friend I have; but I love my Personal Friend so well, as not to abandon, or rail at him, tho' my whole Country fell upon him ... I take my self to be the only Scribler of my Time, of any degree of distinction, who never receiv'd any Places from the Establishment, any Pension from a Court, or any Presents from a Ministry. I desire to preserve this Honour untainted to my Grave.

(Pope to Carteret, 16 February 1723)

Once again a personal restriction had been turned by Pope into an inner freedom, an imputation of treachery into a declaration of his ideals. To withdraw from the world of power and influence was to gain another kind of power which government could not control.

Throughout the 1720s Pope had been attacked in newspapers and pamphlets for his morals, religion and physique. None of these pieces has the control of tone and image, or the underlying moral authority, to deserve the name of satire; but the invective must have stung none the less. Pope bided his time, and in 1728 he reappeared on the literary scene as an original author with two powerful satirical works in prose and verse which signalled to the literary world that he was out of his corner.

The Dunciad appeared amid a swirl of scandal and indignation. This spirited mock-epic vision of a world run mad, starring the luckless Theobald as the leading dunce, settled a number of scores and pictured his enemies as indulging in disgusting acts and childish fantasy-games symbolic of their particular folly or obsession. In the same year he published a prose satire, *The Art of Sinking in Poetry*, a burlesque critical essay and anthology of inept writing, with offenders characterized as appropriate birds, beasts and fishes.

Not surprisingly, the years 1728–9 brought a barrage of attacks in return. J. V. Guerinot's catalogue, *Pamphlet Attacks on Alexander Pope, 1711–1744* (London, 1969), lists 158 items in all (newspapers largely excluded), of which twenty-two belong to the year 1728 and eleven to 1729. *A Popp upon Pope, Sawney, The Popiad, The Female Dunciad, Codrus, or the Dunciad Dissected, The Curliad, Tom o'Bedlam's Dunciad* and *Pope Alexander's Supremacy* are just a few of the more striking. As usual, the publisher Edmund Curll (a shameless purveyor of scandal, dirt and lies) was behind some of them. Summing up the onslaught Pope had to endure throughout his life, Guerinot concludes: 'It is much as though a quarterly magazine devoted entirely to attacks on one author should run for over thirty years.'

As he became a figure of public controversy Pope's domestic life settled into a reassuring routine. It must have highlighted for him a contrast between a world of integrity and good humour within the secure boundaries of private friendship and family responsibilities, and a wider world that was bitter, vicious and dishonest. Somehow symbolic of this was his move in 1719 to Twickenham. His villa by the Thames was handsome, though not grand. From the small back lawn (which still exists) he could watch the river carrying its traffic downstream to London and think of a life that he was consciously distanced from. Here he devoted himself to the care of his mother (who lived to advanced old age) and to the creation of a garden into which he poured considerable energy and creativeness. As the years passed it grew under his hands into a landscape of varied moods and tones, a place of refreshment and contemplation where nature and art were brought into harmony. Between the landscaped garden and the house was the road to Hampton Court, and running beneath it Pope formed an elaborate grotto decorated with shells, mirrors, small waterfalls and a lamp to create glittering light effects. In this Cave of Fancy, expressive perhaps of his more imaginative self, Pope liked to sit. It is clear from his *Epistle to Burlington* (1731) that he considered architecture and gardening as important artistic activities, and that he regarded a person's setting as symbolic of his inner life. No wonder Pope felt that his house, garden and grotto represented in part the landscape of his own mind.

Physically restricted as he was, Pope none the less enjoyed a summer routine of rambles and visits. He had a circle of aristocratic friends whom he admired for their honesty, taste or personal warmth, who were disengaged from the world of politics and city corruption, and who also had beautiful gardens. Lord Burlington, patron of the arts and influential amateur architect, was his neighbour at Chiswick House, a handsome palladian villa where poets, musicians and artists were welcomed, and where the gardens were being shaped in the more natural style Pope was pursuing at Twickenham. Another friend and regular host was Lord Cobham, whose famous grounds at Stowe featured temples and groves commemorating great men of the past, a kind of moralizing landscape ('paysage moralisé') where Pope could view his own bust within a 'Temple of British Worthies'. A particularly devoted admirer was Lord Bathurst, a man in whose company Pope could unwind and whose boundless energy and unstinting appetites (for drink, food and sex) did not prevent (or perhaps ensured) his living to be ninety-one; his country estate of Cirencester Park benefited much from Pope's advice with building and planting, and a small summer-house known as 'Pope's seat' can still be seen there.

Pope enshrined these friendships in three of his so-called 'Moral Essays'. The *Epistle to Burlington* (1731) celebrates natural taste and ridicules the grotesque excesses of the wealthy fool; the *Epistle to Cobham* (1734) explores human 'character' and the possibility of pinning down something that is essentially paradoxical and changeable; and the *Epistle to Bathurst* (1733) sets the city world of financial corruption against one man's charitable benevolence. In each case the particular quality of Pope's admiration for the addressee makes itself felt (nicely varied according to the man), and this establishes a norm of honesty and openness against which satiric judgements can be made.

Pope's model for this approach was the Roman poet Horace. In the work of his ancient predecessor he recognized a sympathetic spirit who celebrated a life of honest retirement and good-humoured virtue. Horace invoked and addressed his friends, whom he saw as embodying a genuine humane integrity, and against them he placed the world of folly, pride and self-seeking. Horace offered Pope a voice and method that fitted his own situation, and it was in the various *Imitations of Horace* published between 1733 and 1738 that Pope spoke out with confidence against the corruption that he felt was seeping down through society.

The source of this national corruption was the Prime Minister Sir Robert Walpole. At least this was the view of the increasingly vocal opposition, swelled after 1733 by the 'opposition Whigs' who had broken with Walpole over his Excise Bill. At their heart were the 'Patriots', a group of talented young politicians (including William Pitt and three nephews of Lord Cobham) who gathered around the rival court of the Prince of Wales, now an enemy of his father, the King. They were influenced in their thinking by the patriotic ideals of Lord Bolingbroke, and their confidence was increased by the contributions made to their cause by poets and dramatists for whom 'Virtue' and 'Liberty' were the watchwords: any references to Greek democracy or the moral ideals of ancient Rome were sure to make a political point.

A shrewd and generally capable man, Walpole had held the reins of power since 1721, favoured by George I, and George II and Queen Caroline. His determination to maintain order in the kingdom (another Jacobite Rising was always possible – and indeed happened in 1745) was an obsession with him, and by the late 1730s he had developed a widespread and intricate system of informers, placemen and journalists who were secretly in his pay. These included, as we now know, John Curll and 'Orator' Henley, both relentless Pope-baiters. Walpole himself had become suspicious, short-tempered, jealous of any rival, a person confident of his own abilities and yet anxious to surround himself with mediocre flatterers and yes-men – people of talent and integrity had been forced out. The *Imitations of Horace*, therefore, hit their mark and Walpole himself drew some of Pope's most direct and pointed satire. Government annoyance increased, but a turning-point came with Pope's unashamed address to Bolingbroke in his imitation of *Epistle I.i* (1738). The wrath of the government newspapers was released. The Prime

Minister's nod had obviously been given, and from this point on the journals and gazettes hounded Pope more than ever.

One attack (and perhaps the one with the best claim to literary merit) struck home more than the others. This was the anonymous *Verses Address'd to the Imitator of Horace* (1733). The poem ended with the following curse:

> Like the first bold Assassin's be thy Lot,
> Ne'er be thy Guilt forgiven, or forgot;
> But as thou hate'st, be hated by Mankind,
> And with the Emblem of thy crooked Mind,
> Mark'd on thy Back, like *Cain*, by God's own Hand;
> Wander like him, accursed through the Land.

The author was Lady Mary Wortley Montagu, who believed herself to be the 'Sappho' of Pope's imitation of Horace *Satire II.i* ('P-x'd by her Love, or libell'd by her Hate'). She seems to have had help from her ally Lord Hervey (soon to be featured as 'Sporus' in *Epistle to Arbuthnot*), but the main thrust of the attack was hers.

Daughter of the Duke of Kingston, Lady Mary had in her youth been the toast of the literary salons for her intelligence and beauty (until damaged by the smallpox), and as a young wife she had entranced Pope, whose feelings for her grew stronger when her diplomat-husband took her off to Constantinople. In fact Pope's letters to her during 1716–18 are extraordinary for their sharp observation, warmth of tone, and their occasionally unsettling visions. *Eloisa to Abelard*, which he sent her in 1717, seems to catch the feverishness of his feelings for this remote impossible love, especially when Eloisa imagines a future poet 'In sad similitude of griefs to mine,/Condemn'd whole years in absence to deplore,/And image charms he must behold no more' (360–62). But Pope's feelings, like Eloisa's, led nowhere. At some point their friendship strained and broke. One account describes a proposal of marriage when the poet's declaration of love was met by uncontrollable laughter. Whatever the cause of the rift, by 1733 their mutual dislike was total and thereafter 'Sappho' makes regular guest-appearances in his satire.

Some of Pope's finest writing is about women, and we should recall the prominence of female figures in his work (ranging from Belinda, Eloisa and the Unfortunate Lady, to the goddess Dulness and the pageant of women in *Epistle to a Lady*). Also some of his most brilliant letters were written to female correspondents. Like many of his contemporaries Pope associated women with a powerful imagination, not always under control, and when he writes of women his verse often records the imagination's ability to explore a colourful and more visionary world, with effects ranging through the dazzling and kaleidoscopic to the grotesque and tragic.

One woman in Pope's life, however, represented for him the stability of true affection. Martha Blount (the 'Lady' of his *Epistle to a Lady*) had been a friend since Pope's late teens. She and her sister (the darker, more vivacious Teresa) came from an impoverished Catholic family living at Mapledurham Manor on the Thames near Reading. Pope's feelings were first stirred by Teresa, but it was Martha on whom Pope came to rely for good humour, constancy, and the kind of calm inner radiance Pope captures so well in the moon image which lights her appearance in his poem (lines 249–56). She represents that principle of integrity which recurs as a positive throughout his poetry; for him it is a genuine wholeness of being, an ability to sustain an inner honesty which is not self-enclosing, but radiates to friends, society and the world while never compromising the principles within.

The extension of the self outwards so that self-love becomes social love is one of the controlling ideas of Pope's *Essay on Man* (1733–4). This was originally planned to be the first part of an ambitious poetic project, a great work mapping out the scope of human knowledge and the nature of society in its civil and religious aspects, and considering a whole range of associated questions of human behaviour and social morality. This so-called 'opus magnum', projected in four books of epistles, soon became unwieldy and the material was suitably dispersed into the 'Moral Essays' and, in a more scattered way, into *The Dunciad* and the *Imitations of Horace*. *An Essay on Man*, however, encapsulates the aims and materials of what would have been a kind of philosophical epic.

On publication Pope took great pains to conceal his authorship of the poem, and he watched with delight as so many of his enemies praised the work as a grand and inspiring *tour de force* much above anything the great Pope could manage. Even his adversaries, therefore, were forced to admire it, and it soon carried its author's fame across Europe, as the many translations testify. But in 1737 it ran into trouble when a Swiss Professor, Jean-Pierre de Crousaz, published a repudiation of Pope's ideas (based, it must be said, on a very unreliable translation). Pope's enemies in England soon saw their opportunity to attack his supposedly heretical ideas, with Curll again figuring prominently. Fortunately Pope had a defender to hand in William Warburton, an ambitious theologian and controversialist. Warburton's *Vindication* of the *Essay* had its effect and its author soon became Pope's friend and protector, and eventually his literary executor. As his life drew to a close Pope faced the daunting task of attempting to republish his *Works* in a suitably final form, and it was Warburton who pushed the enterprise forward with relish. Pope allowed him scope with supplying explanatory footnotes, and the 'authorial' notes to *An Essay on Criticism*, the 'Moral Essays' and *The Dunciad* still bear witness to their collaboration. How far some of these represent Warburton's views rather than Pope's is open to question.

An equally warm friendship (and one with more positive results for lovers of Pope today) grew up with Joseph Spence, a young man who had come to Pope's notice in 1726 through his intelligent yet critical appraisal of the *Odyssey* translation. Spence's points are judicious and scholarly and Pope recognized the truth of many of them. It is to his credit that he appreciated this honest, constructive criticism and made the author his devoted friend. Towards the end of his life it was to Spence that Pope confided many opinions, thoughts and memories, which his friend duly recorded. Spence's *Anecdotes*, now available in a well-edited modern edition, provide an invaluable insight into Pope's character.

It is partly through Spence, who was in constant attendance, that we view Pope's last days when the 'long disease' of his life was coming to an end. It is, above all, a sociable scene, with friends old and new coming to take their leave. One young visitor recalled:

On Monday last I took my everlasting Farewell of him ... The same social Kindness, the same friendly Concern for those he loved, even in the minutest Instances, that had distinguished his Heart through Life, were uppermost in his Thoughts to the last.

Pope's life and work are intimately connected, and it is perhaps friendship which provides the most important thread. So much of his writing has reference to, and is shaped by, particular friends who seem to draw out one part of his complex personality. The openness and variety of his friendships are a key to many aspects of his art: his mastery of subtle shifts of tone, his ability to widen out the personal detail (*even in the minutest Instances* . . .) into a truth about human nature; perhaps above all his sense that at the centre of every endeavour (whether in writing, gardening or in human relationships) there should be a core of humanity, a living principle, at work. The compressed power of Pope's poetry lies here.

2. The Techniques of Pope's Verse

The vast majority of Pope's poems are written in the form of the heroic couplet, that is, in iambic pentameters rhymed in pairs. It is easy to become overwhelmed by technicalities when attempting any formal description of the way poetry sounds. Stress and rhythm are elusive things, and verse works best when it strains against order and regularity. But Pope was a conscious craftsman in his handling of the heroic couplet, and the pleasure of reading him is greatly increased if we are aware of the subtlety and flexibility with which he uses his verse-form, since it is an integral part of the meaning of his poetry. Once we have covered the most basic elements we begin to see a whole world of sound and meaning opening up, and the poems gain a new dimension. In the following remarks I make no attempt to be comprehensive, and the final judge must always be the reader's own ear.

An iambic is a stressed syllable preceded by an unstressed syllable, i.e. the sound ti-*tum* (as in the word *above*), and a pentameter is a line with five stresses. A strict iambic pentameter, therefore, would be:

> Above, below, without, within, around

(In case that sounds like nonsense I should point out that it is line 458 of Pope's *The Temple of Fame*!) But when we say that a poem is in 'iambic pentameters' we do not mean that every line is regular. If it were, then it would be excruciatingly tedious. No, what we are describing by the term 'iambic pentameter' is only the underlying *pulse*. The *rhythm* of the poem is made up of the subtle variations of stress as we read (and which every reader may hear differently). Take the following couplet as an example:

> Let humble Allen, with an aukward Shame,
> Do good by stealth, and blush to find it Fame
> (*Epilogue to the Satires*, Dial. 1, 135–6)

We feel the iambic pulse, and the second line is very regular with the stress falling on each of the important words. But the first line is a little different. Though *with* is in the position of a stressed syllable, it is surely a very weak one, with the result that the line falls easily into two halves consisting of the balanced phrases *humble Allen* and *aukward Shame*,

15

encouraging us to note a relationship between them. (We have only to alter the line to: *Let humble Allen feel an aukward Shame* to sense that an unnecessary heaviness has crept in.)

Pope can achieve, when he wishes, a deliberate smoothness and harmony:

> To Rules of Poetry no more confin'd,
> I learn to smooth and harmonize my Mind
> *(Imitations of Horace*, Epistle II.2, 202–3)

Here the regularity of the second line conveys the very feeling Pope describes, just as the first line (thanks to the word *Poetry*) does not fully confine itself to the five stresses; indeed among the ten syllables there seem to be only three really heavy stresses, falling on the three words (Rules, Poetry, confin'd) which carry the weight of meaning.

Already, I suspect, some readers may be protesting that they hear the sounds differently. Whatever the case, it is important that we are aware of what we are 'hearing' as we read. Pope's poetry loses more than most by not being heard, and as our eyes run over the couplets from rhyme to rhyme, it is all too easy to move down the lines without registering the vigour and subtlety of the sound. Until we become accustomed to 'hearing' Pope as we silently read him, we may find that our eyes skip along too quickly, or that we concentrate too much on deciphering the sense. We have to train ourselves to settle into the pulse of the verse and feel the intricate rhythms playing across it.

One poem in which pulse and rhythm play an important part is *Eloisa to Abelard*, where Pope is able to chart the ebb and flow of the speaker's passions, particularly at those moments when her 'pulse that riots' (line 252) imposes its own patterns on the verse, as in the following lines:

> No, fly me, fly me! far as Pole from Pole;
>
> (289)

and

> Ah come not, write not, think not once of me
>
> (291)

In each case, after an opening syllable of exclamation we suddenly find that the iambic pulse has been reversed (*tum*-ti, *tum*-ti), reflecting how her passions have broken the bounds and are asserting a counter-stress.

An issue closely related to that of rhythm is the phrasing of the pentameter line, and Pope's skill in this is considerable. One danger of the heroic couplet is monotony, and Pope is usually very careful to handle his phrasing in such a way that the verse does not become predictable. When as a young man he composed his *Pastorals* he declared in his preface 'On Pastoral Poetry' that 'As for the numbers themselves [i.e. the metre], tho' they are properly of the heroic measure, they should be the smoothest, the most easy and flowing imaginable', and some of the poem's finest lines show how Pope could achieve such smoothness without monotony. Here the shepherd Alexis is addressing his absent love:

> *Where-e'er you walk*, cool Gales shall fan the Glade,
> Trees, *where you sit*, shall crowd into a Shade,
> *Where-e'er you tread*, the blushing Flow'rs shall rise,
> And all things flourish *where you turn your Eyes*.

> (*Summer*, 73–6)

The effect is extremely simple, but works beautifully. The echoing phrases (in italics) shift place within the lines as if mimicking the girl's movements as she walks, sits, and turns.

Another genre in which simplicity is appropriate is the epitaph, but here it is combined with a more formal dignity. Pope's twelve-line *Epitaph. On Mr Gay. In Westminster-Abbey* is a good example of the way the verse technique is an integral part of a poem's meaning, and once again it is important to be alert to the subtlety of the phrasing. It begins:

> Of Manners gentle, of Affections mild;
> In Wit, a Man; Simplicity, a Child;

> (1–2)

In the above couplet the phrases are disposed in pairs, with no verbs; everything is finely balanced and keeps a decorum that is part of his tribute to his subject.

> With native Humour temp'ring virtuous Rage,
> Form'd to delight at once and lash the age;

> (3–4)

Here *native Humour* and *virtuous Rage* are 'tempered' by the central verb. But the second line has to work harder to hold its contrasting ideas in balance (*to delight . . . and lash*). It suggests that Gay's delight is spontaneous (*to delight at once*), but then we realize that *at once* here also means 'simultaneously', and that Pope is saying Gay both delighted and at the same time attacked his society. *Lash* and *Rage* reinforce each other and introduce a note of passion which complicates the mildness and simplicity of the opening couplet.

> Above Temptation, in a low Estate,
> And uncorrupted, ev'n among the Great;
>
> (5–6)

This third couplet works through several contrasts: *Above . . . low, Temptation . . . uncorrupted, low Estate . . . the Great,* and it clearly sets a social scale against a moral scale, with ironic effect (what is low in the one may be high in the other).

> A safe Companion, and an easy Friend,
> Unblam'd thro' Life, lamented in thy End.
>
> (7–8)

Here Pope focuses on Gay's private relationships, and the balanced stresses recall the opening couplet; once again we feel *safe* and *easy* as we read these lines which celebrate Gay's *Life* and lament his *End.* The clear break within the line is called a caesura, and the following line 9 provides a particularly strong one by way of exclamation:

> These are Thy Honours! not that here thy Bust
> Is mix'd with Heroes, or with Kings
>
> (9–10)

As if to emphasize the exclamation, the rest of line 9 runs on into the next (a technique known as enjambement). We are back among the Great, but again only ironically, because line 10 ends with the words:

> thy dust;

(a reminder that comes with a slight shock to complete the phrase). The poem's final couplet now brings forward the *Worthy* and the *Good* (as if in contrast to heroes and kings):

> But that the Worthy and the Good shall say,
> Striking their pensive bosoms –
>
> (11–12)

And this last phrase acts as a kind of parenthesis, suspending the final statement and allowing only three syllables for their spoken tribute:

> *Here* lies GAY.

And so the poem ends, not with any fulsome flattery, but with the words on his stone tablet stripped bare of any further compliments, but with a new personal emphasis (*Here* is within *their pensive bosoms*). The epitaph concludes with this limiting and narrowing down to the fact of death, but we see how Pope's masterly lines, while recalling Gay the social satirist and friend of the Great, find their home in human intimacy. The poem combines a public pronouncement with a private memory.

This epitaph is, I think, a good example of how the techniques of Pope's verse carry the meaning of a poem. Particularly noteworthy are the rhymes, always placed on a strong and telling word, secure in emphasis and somehow final. This is vividly illustrated by the fact that we can reconstruct the poem merely from the powerful rhyme-words, as follows:

> *Mild* as a *child*
> He *raged* at the *age*,
> Shunned *great estate*;
> A *friend* to the *end*,
> His *bust* and *dust*
> *Say* here lies *Gay*.

In couplet-writing rhyme is obviously an important resource, and here Pope is putting his rhyming words to work very effectively. The significance of these and the interplay between them is often a revealing pointer to the quality of the writing. My little invented poem highlights, I think, how effectively they work here.

When used for satiric purposes rhyme can exploit its ability to bring different ideas together:

> Nine years! cries he, who high in *Drury-lane*
> Lull'd by soft Zephyrs thro' the *broken Pane*
>
> (*Epistle to Arbuthnot*, 41–2)

Across the rhyme the perspective cruelly shifts, from large to small, from the public world to the private, from the poverty-stricken poet's dreams of success to the chill wind of reality.

Sometimes the interplay of meaning in a rhyme can make its own unspoken ironic comment, as it seems to do when the frantic Eloisa describes her dreams:

> Then conscience sleeps, and leaving nature free,
> All my loose soul unbounded springs to thee.
>
> (*Eloisa to Abelard*, 227–8)

The energetic freedom of the second line (*loose, unbounded, springs*) climaxes in the word *thee*. But this is the very thing that is imprisoning Eloisa (her obsession with her former lover Abelard – the *thee* of the poem). By setting *free* against *thee*, the rhyme reminds us how all her gestures of release and freedom reach the same dead-end in the image of her absent lover. What looks at first like a declaration of independence is shown to be the opposite.

The word 'balance' has already occurred several times, and indeed the resources of rhyme and rhythm within the heroic-couplet form are ideal for expressing concepts of poise and order. In the following lines from *An Essay on Man*, for example, the poet's point about the interplay of passions in the human mind is presented in a balanced way that suggests Pope has thoughtfully weighed the matter:

> Love, Hope, and Joy, fair pleasure's smiling train,
> Hate, Fear, and Grief, the family of pain;
> These mix'd with art, and to due bounds confin'd,
> Make and maintain the balance of the mind

(ii, 117–20)

This carefully structured passage sets in opposition the various passions of pleasure and of pain, but confines them to their due bounds and achieves a balance between them. We have here, in fact, both *opposition* (between lines 1 and 2) and *apposition* (within each of those lines).

It is in such a context of balance and order that the heroic-couplet form permits every emotional nuance to make itself felt. Far from being a constriction, its tight rein registers the slightest movement. As a medium for satire the heroic couplet allows the most intricate possibilities. Its regularity and poise highlight any kind of deviation, and it implicitly sets up a norm against which error may be measured. We shall see in a moment some of the satirical possibilities of this, but it would be wrong to think of Pope's verse as rigid, schoolmasterly and judgemental. We should rather think of it in terms of a force-field which allows us to plot out relationships, assess values and consider contradictions and ironies. Pope sets up such a force-field in these two separate lines from *An Essay on Criticism*, the first about the ideal critic, the second about the great Roman poet Horace:

> Modestly bold, and Humanly severe

(636)

and

> Yet judg'd with Coolness tho' he sung with Fire

(659)

Each line has both apposition and opposition. The first measures boldness and severity by a humane modesty; the second brings the heat of creativity up against a cooler critical judgement. Pope does not want these apparent extremes to cancel each other out – on the contrary, he sees a positive value in their interaction.

Moving towards the world of satire we can see how such techniques of apposition can be used to make an ironic point. In the following couplet Pope is describing the fate of a young lady sent back to the country after the social whirl of London:

> She went, to plain-work, and to purling brooks,
> Old-fashion'd halls, dull aunts, and croaking rooks
>> (*Epistle to Miss Blount, on her leaving the Town,*
>> *after the Coronation*, 11–12)

The *purling brooks* (a commonplace of pastoral poetry) have been replaced by the more realistic *croaking rooks* (a very different sound) and the *dull aunts* have become as much a part of the deadly routine as the embroidered *plain-work*. The couplet brings all these details crowding together and allows us to play one off against the other.

Such juxtapositions within the context of satirical attack can be a deadly weapon, as in Pope's characterization of Atossa:

> From loveless youth to unrespected age,
> No Passion gratify'd except her Rage.
> So much the Fury still out-ran the Wit,
> The Pleasure miss'd her, and the Scandal hit.
>> (*Epistle to a Lady*, 125–8)

From the chilling polarities of the first line (which condenses the whole span of her adult life) we are given a series of appositions: *Passion* and *Rage*, *Fury* and *Wit*, *Pleasure* and *Scandal*, all those things which trap the foolish woman between extremes. We begin with negatives (*loveless*, *unrespected*, *No* Passion), then move to the single positive (*except her Rage*) which turns out to be her only satisfaction, and a pointless one at that; then on to her inability to reach goals or targets (*out-ran*, *miss'd*), once again climaxed by an ironic success (*the Scandal hit*). In this example we see apposition achieving satiric force (made all the more powerful by the constant presence of a background order and regularity) as though a chaotic life has been stripped of all its excuses and self-deceptions and set out starkly before us.

Sometimes the appositions are less polarized, so that they create an image of confusion, as in the case of the lady:

21

> who in sweet vicissitude appears
> Of Mirth and Opium, Ratafie and Tears
>
> (*Epistle to a Lady*, 109–10)

The word *vicissitude* suggests not just that the drugs confuse her mind (Ratafie was a kind of cherry brandy), but also that the effects of them can be mistaken for her own emotions, and these confusions are captured by the alternating terms in the second line. Is she happy, or is it the opium? Is she sad, or is it the brandy?

Apposition can also be used in satire to suggest that a person's values have become distorted, or that society has lost its sense of value entirely, as in the following lines from *The Rape of the Lock* describing the various disasters that may befall a young society woman:

> Whether the Nymph shall break *Diana*'s Law,
> Or some frail *China* Jar receive a Flaw,
> Or stain her Honour, or her new Brocade,
> Forget her Pray'rs, or miss a Masquerade,
> Or lose her Heart, or Necklace, at a Ball;
> Or whether Heav'n has doom'd that *Shock* must fall.
>
> (ii, 105–10)

The balance of these lines places *Brocade* and *Honour*, *Heart* and *Necklace*, on an equal level, an effect achieved by what is termed zeugma: making two contrasting terms the objects of the same verb (here *stain* and *lose*). The most famous example of zeugma in the poem is the line describing Queen Anne, who:

> Dost sometimes Counsel take – and sometimes *Tea*.
>
> (iii, 8)

A more complex use of apposition can bring images together in an uneasy or disturbing way. In *Epistle to a Lady*, for example, Pope juxtaposes

> Sappho's diamonds with her dirty smock,
> Or Sappho at her toilet's greasy task,
> With Sappho fragrant at an ev'ning Mask:
>
> (24–6)

In the context of dirt and grease the word *fragrant* makes us feel distinctly uncomfortable. Here Pope also uses the technique of alliteration (repetition of the same consonant) to link the words *diamonds* and *dirty*. Were we to alter the phrase to *Sappho's diamonds with her filthy smock* the effect would be less memorable.

22

Alliteration, in fact, can be an effective means of exposing inconsistencies or incongruities, either by a satirical hammer-blow, or used more sparingly and pointedly. In, either case it can have a devastating effect:

> Proud as a Peeress, prouder as a Punk
> (*Epistle to a Lady*, 70)

or

> Slow rose a form, in majesty of Mud
> (*Dunciad*, ii, 326)

Alliteration can sometimes attempt an imitative sound, as in the following couplet where combined with a laboured stress-pattern the repeated 'c' perhaps suggests the wearisomely exact ticking of a clock:

> Or o'er cold coffee trifle with the spoon,
> Count the slow clock, and dine exact at noon
> (*Epistle to Miss Blount, on her leaving the Town, after the Coronation*, 17–18)

A related device is assonance (repeated vowel sounds), which can likewise be used to draw two words together, as with the echoing 'i' in this line describing the fate of the rich but unhappy Pamela:

> A vain, unquiet, glitt'ring, wretched Thing!
> (*Epistle to Miss Blount, With the Works of Voiture*, 54)

where the word *wretched* seems to break apart a single phrase (*glitt'ring Thing*). At the other extreme, assonance can be used in parody to create a grotesque effect, as it does in the following couplet which mockingly imitates the thudding style of Sir Richard Blackmore's poetry:

> Rend with tremendous Sound your ears asunder,
> With Gun, Drum, Trumpet, Blunderbuss & Thunder
> (*Imitations of Horace*, Satire II, i, 25–6)

As well as expressing obvious sound-effects such as these, Pope is particularly skilled at capturing the rhythms of human speech. This is the angry dandy, Sir Plume, who uses froth and bluster instead of argument:

> With earnest Eyes, and round unthinking Face,
> He first the Snuff-box open'd, then the Case,
> And thus broke out – 'My Lord, why, what the Devil?
> Z—ds! damn the Lock! 'fore Gad, you must be civil!

23

> Plague on't! 'tis past a Jest – nay prithee, Pox!
> Give her the Hair' – he spoke, and rapp'd his Box.
>
> (*The Rape of the Lock*, iv, 125–30)

The rapid percussive phrases are continued non-verbally in the sudden rapping of the snuff-box, and Pope captures Plume's perplexity and incoherence through the build-up of the staccato rhythms and the way in which each line is lamely padded out with exclamations and expletives (*what the Devil?, Z – ds!, 'fore Gad, Plague on 't!, Pox!*).

So far we have considered rhythm, phrasing, rhyme, apposition, alliteration and assonance, and have seen some of the results, satirical and otherwise, that Pope is able to achieve. We must remember, however, that there are dangers in overemphasizing mere sound and in focusing too much on minute local effects. We must try to maintain a balance between the details and the wider meanings, always remembering that Pope himself was suspicious of the kind of poetry that laboured too obviously for mere sound-effects. This is clear from a passage in his *Essay on Criticism* where he laughs at certain excesses, but at the same time shows himself extremely sensitive to the sound of verse and what various techniques can achieve:

> But most by *Numbers* judge a Poet's Song,
> And *smooth* or *rough*, with them, is *right* or *wrong*;
> In the bright *Muse* tho' thousand *Charms* conspire,
> Her *Voice* is all these tuneful Fools admire . . .
> These *Equal Syllables* alone require,
> Tho' oft the Ear the *open Vowels* tire,
> While *Expletives* their feeble Aid *do* join,
> And ten low Words oft creep in one dull Line,
> While they ring round the same *unvary'd Chimes*,
> With sure *Returns* of still *expected Rhymes*.
> Where-e'er you find *the cooling Western Breeze*,
> In the next Line, it *whispers thro' the Trees*;
> If *Chrystal Streams with pleasing Murmurs creep*,
> The Reader's threaten'd (not in vain) with *Sleep*.
> Then, at the *last*, and *only* Couplet fraught
> With some *unmeaning* Thing they call a *Thought*,
> A *needless Alexandrine* ends the Song,
> That like a wounded Snake, drags its slow length along.
>
> (337–57)

The targets of Pope's satire here are those writers who use the various techniques of verse without being aware of the relationship of sound to sense ('The *Sound* must seem an *Eccho* to the *Sense*', as he goes on to say at line 365). Writers like these employ predictable rhymes, fill out their ten syllables with meaningless words (*do* join), and fail to consider the effects of what they do, as when they use a monosyllabic line (*ten low Words* . . .) or an alexandrine (a line of six stresses, imitated by Pope in line 357). Pope certainly does not disapprove of these techniques: it is their misuse, or unthinking use, that he condemns. Both can be very effective if used sparingly and at an appropriate moment, as Pope himself demonstrates. The following procession of ten monosyllables, for example, combined with an overloading of the stress-pattern, conveys the discomfort of visiting Timon's Villa:

> And when up ten steep slopes you've dragg'd your thighs
> *(Epistle to Burlington*, 131)

And in the following passage a final alexandrine, combined with a triplet rhyme (a device used very sparingly by Pope) and well-judged repetitions, vividly enacts the way in which rumour spreads:

> And all who told it, added something new,
> And all who heard it, made Enlargements too,
> In ev'ry Ear it spread, on ev'ry Tongue it grew.
> *(The Temple of Fame*, 470–72)

Repetition and enlargement are here entirely appropriate.

With the exception of the *Epitaph*, we have so far been looking at specific devices and their use, without examining how Pope builds up effects over longer passages. The writer of couplets always has to be careful that the larger effect does not become either repetitive or fragmented, and Pope takes great care over this. The following extract from *The Rape of the Lock* occurs at the moment when Clarissa, the woman of experience, is offering her unwelcome advice to Belinda. It demonstrates well how Pope is able to sustain a line of argument while at the same time giving a good sense of the character of the speaker. Here he has to convey a combination of realism and good humour, because that, after all, is Clarissa's message. Her moralizing is urgent, but must not be allowed to become heavy-handed or 'preachy':

> But since, alas! frail Beauty must decay,
> Curl'd or uncurl'd, since Locks will turn to grey,
> Since painted, or not painted, all shall fade,
> And she who scorns a Man, must die a Maid;
> What then remains, but well our Pow'r to use,
> And keep good Humour still whate'er we lose?

> And trust me, Dear! good Humour can prevail,
> When Airs, and Flights, and Screams, and Scolding fail.
> Beauties in vain their pretty Eyes may roll;
> Charms strike the sight, but Merit wins the Soul.

(v, 25–34)

The secret of success here is Pope's subtle shifting of the tone. 'Tone' is an elusive but vital concept, and is best thought of as 'tone of voice' (the difference, for example, between gentle pleading, anger, excitement, or a sarcastic inflexion). The word *alas*! immediately sets a tone of resignation and sorrow, continued in the final phrases of each of the opening lines: *Beauty must decay*, *Locks will turn to grey*, *all shall fade*. We can picture phrases like these carved on to funeral monuments. But we sense also that a very different tone has crept in: *Curl'd or uncurl'd, painted, or not painted*, a lighter, half-humorous note, slightly mocking Belinda's obsession with her own beauty. There follows Clarissa's inevitable question: *What then remains?*, and we perhaps expect a negative answer. But the complication in the tone should have alerted us to what in fact follows. Clarissa instead asserts woman's power and the necessity of tackling life with good humour and common sense. This is caught in the rhyme of *use* and *lose*, which puts the choice very clearly! In the next line *trust me, Dear!* brings a sudden intimacy with Belinda and (importantly) stops Clarissa sounding like a preacher addressing an audience from a pulpit. Suddenly after generalizing about death's imperative (*must, will, shall, must*) she offers a positive possibility (good Humour *can* prevail), and she offers it more quietly and directly to Belinda herself. Once again the rhyme (this time *prevail* and *fail*) carries the alternatives of her argument, putting into perspective Belinda's *Airs, and Flights, and Screams, and Scolding* (how routine and repetitive they sound!). In the final couplet the beauties' *pretty Eyes* (a deliberately commonplace phrase) are placed in a wider context with *Charms strike the Sight, but Merit wins the Soul*, a line which uses apposition across the caesura to weigh the ideas against each other, here supported by a linking alliteration (between *Sight* and *Soul*) which makes the contrast clear.

In the above passage we see so many of Pope's poetic techniques at work, all helping to reinforce Clarissa's appeal to common sense and good humour. What could have been just a succession of moralizing phrases becomes a sustained argument employing subtle emotional tactics.

In the long extract from *An Essay on Criticism* quoted earlier it was clear that Pope had a very sensitive ear for the sound-effects of verse, and that in making fun of other poets' excesses he was lamenting their *misuse* of a valuable resource. In order to gain some idea of the power sound can have when harnessed to meaning, we have only to look at the passage from *The Rape of the Lock* in which Pope describes the sylphs hovering round Belinda as she sails down the river. It is a sound-picture of great complexity which achieves a simple and direct effect:

> Some to the Sun their Insect-Wings unfold,
> Waft on the Breeze, or sink in Clouds of Gold.
> Transparent Forms, too fine for mortal Sight,
> Their fluid Bodies half dissolv'd in Light.
> Loose to the Wind their airy Garments flew,
> Thin glitt'ring Textures of the filmy Dew;
> Dipt in the richest Tincture of the Skies,
> Where Light disports in ever-mingling Dies,
> While ev'ry Beam new transient Colours flings,
> Colours that change whene'er they wave their Wings.

> (ii, 59–68)

The sylphs are disembodied airy creatures, and in order to suggest their very elusive presence Pope employs the lightest of sounds, especially the 'i', which is a thin sound (as opposed to the rounder open vowels), and the liquid effect of the repeated 'l'. (The two are often combined, as in *fluid, dissolv'd, glitt'ring, filmy, mingling* or *flings*.) The alliteration on other consonants is subtly done, and is spread through the whole passage rather than confined to particular lines. This has the effect of creating a general harmoniousness. A limited number of consonants strike up an echo from one word to another: *Some, Sun, sink, Sight, Skies; Wings, Waft, Wind, wave, Wings; Clouds, Colours; Gold, Garments, glitt'ring; Transparent, Textures, Tincture, transient; Forms, fine, fluid, flew, filmy, flings; Breeze, Bodies, Beam; Dew, Dipt, Dies, dissolv'd, disports; Light, Loose, Light*. The result is a kind of tapestry of sound, the aural strands interweaving one with another, mimicking the play of the sylphs in the air. (It could be said, in fact, that sound is the most important element in the passage's meaning.)

But the sylphs are not to be trusted, and Pope's sound-picture has a carefully calculated frivolity about it, even a suggestion of self-indulgence, which is all part of the reader's complex response to the sylphs and what they represent.

To end this brief introduction to some of Pope's poetic techniques I want to look at a paragraph from *An Essay on Man* as an example of how the resources of heroic couplet verse can help support a philosophical argument.

In these lines Pope is bringing to a climax his remarks about the interconnectedness of creation and the forces which operate in it:

> God loves from Whole to Parts: but human soul
> Must rise from Individual to the Whole.
> Self-love but serves the virtuous mind to wake,
> As the small pebble stirs the peaceful lake;
> The centre mov'd, a circle strait succeeds,
> Another still, and still another spreads,
> Friend, parent, neighbour, first it will embrace,
> His country next, and next all human race,
> Wide and more wide, th'o'erflowings of the mind
> Take ev'ry creature in, of ev'ry kind;
> Earth smiles around, with boundless bounty blest,
> And Heav'n beholds its image in his breast.

(iv, 361–72)

Pope is discussing the relationship of the whole to the parts, and such a relationship is evident throughout this passage. In the second line the rhyme-word *Whole* is unavoidably an anticlimax: God has pre-empted such wholeness in line 1, and man's activity must be to labour through the succeeding lines until Heaven and the human come together at the end of the paragraph (*And Heav'n beholds its image in his breast*). The passage charts how the human mind spreads its sympathies outwards from the self to embrace all creation. The rhyme-word *wake* begins the progress, taking us to the *lake*, which will be the controlling image as movements begin to work across it (*small pebble . . . stirs peaceful*). The word *stirs* nicely conveys the idea of being inwardly and emotionally roused (where *strike* would lack this suggestion); similarly, *mov'd* and *embrace* are also emotive as well as technical words. In line 366 the tempo accelerates with a chiasmus (an arching A–B–B–A pattern: *Another still*, and *still another*), which is repeated two lines later (*His country next*, and *next* all *human race*). By line 369 the rhythm is straining against the confines of the couplet (*Wide* and *more* wide), and one line is overflowing into the next (*th'overflowings of the mind Take ev'ry creature in*). By the final couplet Pope can risk a daring combination of alliteration and assonance to drive home the roundness and wholeness of life (*Earth smiles around, with boundless bounty blest*).

Just as Pope in this passage sees meaning and understanding rippling outwards from the small part to the greater whole, so we can appreciate how his poetic technique works out from the tiniest detail to the wider theme. Many of the effects I have described will make themselves felt without conscious detailed analysis, and sometimes it may seem that we have been using a microscope rather than our own eyes. Nevertheless we are surely justified in attempting to understand the mechanisms of Pope's art, and perhaps we are not qualified to pontificate about the boundless bounty of his 'meaning' until we have followed some of the ripples spreading across the lake.

3. *An Essay on Criticism*

'A *little Learning* is a dang'rous Thing', 'To err is *Humane*; to Forgive, *Divine*', 'For *Fools* rush in where *Angels* fear to tread'. The quotations (all from *An Essay on Criticism*) have become part of the English language, and we can see that they all touch on the same theme: presumption, risking danger or error, embarking on some task that is hazardous and demanding. Human capacities are measured against the divine, but danger lies as much in limitation ('A *little Learning*') as in daring to exceed limits ('*Fools* rush in'). It is no surprise that *An Essay on Criticism*, the precocious work of a young man of twenty-two, should have aroused thoughts like these. To attempt a verse-essay on the subject of poetry and criticism, modelled on Horace's *Ars Poetica*, was a bold enterprise for a person who as yet had no independent publication behind him (his *Pastorals* of 1709 had appeared as part of a miscellany volume). The poem prescribes, advises and criticizes, and offers itself as the distilled wisdom of long experience. No wonder that the young Pope keeps returning to images of danger, risk-taking and error!

The idea of risk-taking and the crossing of boundaries links up with a central theme of the poem. To what extent should art be restrained by common sense, judgement, or the 'rules' of writing? Or is poetry a matter of genius, instinct and invention? This tension between the creative impulse and those principles that guide and restrain is an idea that runs throughout Pope's poem, and in tackling the question he was entering into an age-old debate that was still a living issue in 1711. To see where he stands it may be helpful to sketch out the critical context in which Pope was writing, and especially to say something about three of the great classical documents which lie behind *An Essay on Criticism*: Aristotle's *Poetics*, Horace's *Ars Poetica* and Longinus's *On the Sublime*.

(i) The Critical Context

By the early eighteenth century the name of Aristotle (384–322 BC) had become practically synonymous with 'The Rules'. His recommendations in the *Poetics* had been hardened by Renaissance critics into regulations. For example, his discussion of dramatic structure and plausibility (concluding that a tragedy should have a single unified action) had become enshrined as the 'Three Unities' of Time, Place and Action (a single plot, in a single place, lasting no more than twenty-four hours). Such rigorous neoclassical law-giving was particularly entrenched in seventeenth-century France, so that when a great dramatist like Corneille wrote a play spreading the twenty-four hours over two days, the result was scandal, pandemonium, a war of pamphlets and even government involvement. Aristotle's founding principle is that Poetry is an Imitation or Representation. Poetry, therefore, has to be judged according to how well it represents some reality or purpose outside itself. It is not an independent creative power expressing its own reality, but is descriptive of, responsible for, and subordinate to, our 'real-life' experiences, and should be assessed in those terms. For Aristotle, the truths of poetry are universal and general, and should therefore be communicated clearly, convincingly and morally. Criticism is the business of judging how well these aims have been carried through.

Aristotle's assumption about the imitative (or 'mimetic') function of poetry also lies behind Horace's *Ars Poetica* (composed about 12 BC). This is a letter in verse, written in an easy, rather informal style, and offering advice to a young nobleman who is about to embark on some literary project. (Pope's line: 'Men must be *taught* as if you taught them *not*' (574) nicely captures the manner of Horace's poem, and associates it with his own.) Horace is pleasing, instructive, graceful and entertaining, and the principle to which he keeps returning throughout the *Ars Poetica* is the notion of 'decorum', or appropriateness. This involves the relating of the parts to the whole, and the use of a style suitable to a poem's subject (so that the language of epic will be very different from that of pastoral or elegy). Linked to this is the importance of avoiding irrelevance, shapelessness, confusion, or mere self-indulgence. The best writing, says Horace, demands a great deal of correction and revision, and the poet should study the Ancient Greek writers (especially Homer) as suitable models. The qualities Horace stresses in the writer are a sound understanding, shrewd judgement and good sense. All in all, it reads like thoroughly useful advice, and Horace's own style is expressive, persuasive, and beautifully adapted to his argument.

In the mid-seventeenth century critics 're-discovered' another classical authority which gave a rather different emphasis to the topic of poetic creation. This was the fragmentary prose treatise (probably dating from the first century AD) entitled *Peri Hypsous*. The title is usually translated as *On the Sublime*, but is literally 'On Soaring, or Flying High', the opposite being *Peri Bathous*. (In 1728 Pope published a parody-treatise entitled *Peri Bathous: or The Art of Sinking in Poetry*.) The unknown author of this fragmentary document is known as Longinus, though this is unlikely to have been his name. It suddenly came to the notice of writers and critics after its translation from the original Greek into French by Nicolas Boileau in 1674. (In the same year Boileau also published an influential adaptation of Horace's poem, entitled *L'Art Poétique*.) Where Aristotle and Horace stressed how the poet entertains and instructs his reader, Longinus declares in his first chapter:

Whatever transports us with wonder is more effective than something which merely persuades or pleases us. When we are being persuaded we are usually in control, but Sublimity has an irresistible power over us . . A well-aimed stroke of Sublimity scatters everything before it like a thunderflash, and the poet is revealed in all his power.

'Sublimity' focuses on the poet as a transmitter of divine power, an inspired author who is able to seize directly the imagination of the reader or listener. It cannot be sustained throughout a work, but instead special-izes in brief flashes of genius, powerful strokes of imagination. Where Horace advises a young would-be poet on his career, Longinus offers a kind of handbook for a writer to impress his audience. Horace stresses the whole, Longinus highlights the brilliant moments. Both are conscious of how poetry can achieve its effects, but Longinus moves the debate into an elemental context: the sublime poet is godlike and attempts 'the highest flights'; he brings to life the whole universe and satisfies the soul's craving for infinity, for anything that sweeps us beyond the boun-daries of our understanding, and his image is the volcanic eruption of Mount Etna, a fire shrouded in darkness. Human beings, he says, value the extraordinary, but scorn what is merely useful.

We can see immediately the extent to which Longinus stands apart from the Aristotelian tradition. Where Aristotle and Horace tend to stress poetry's responsibility towards the nature of human experience (its appropriateness, correctness, and self-consistency), Longinus places stress on the way art flirts with danger, inspires, transports and explores. Aristotle and Horace value guidelines and the shaping of the material; Longinus delights in the raw material itself, and in the transgressing of boundaries: 'The whole universe is not enough to satisfy our minds . . . our ideas often reach beyond the frontiers that enclose us.'

It would be wrong to see these two traditions as totally opposed to each other (Aristotle and Horace valued creativity and genius, and Lon-ginus valued artistic judgement and the imitation of Homer); nevertheless there is a stark contrast in emphasis and imagery between them: the terminology of the one tends to stress guidelines, structure, decorum, truth-to-nature, responsibility, correctness; and the other emphasizes inspiration, soaring flight, instinctiveness, exploration and boundlessness. In *An Essay on Criticism* Pope is clearly aware of the tensions between these two viewpoints, and for us to understand his poem we need to keep both traditions in mind while we watch him negotiating between the claims of form and energy.

But Pope did not merely have great classical models before him. The critical debate of the previous fifty years also played a part in his thinking and provided him with some direct models for his verse essay. His eminent predecessor as a critic-poet, John Dryden (1631–1700), had dealt in some of his critical essays with the relationship of neoclassical criticism to native English literature. After 1660, with the Restoration of Charles II, French culture, and along with it French critical ideas, rapidly established themselves in England. By the 1690s the critical debate was being fought very much according to the 'Rules'. An influential critic such as Thomas Rymer (in his *Short View of Tragedy*, 1693) could launch the most vitriolic attack on Shakespeare's *Othello* for 'neglecting' so many of the rules. Dryden for one felt that Rymer's rigid approach was inadequate, and he sketched out a response (which he never published) challenging the notion of prescribed rules. However, in his eventual published reply he accepted the Aristotelian line and proceeded to apply the rules thoroughly himself. It is as though he had glimpsed a terrifying void with no authority or regulation. Yet at the climax of his piece he felt able to bring Shakespeare forward as a triumphant exception ('Great Wits sometimes may *gloriously offend*', as Pope says in his *Essay*, 152) who might in the end be pardoned for his moments of brilliance and his truth to nature. Dryden's uneasy acceptance of 'the Rules' should be a useful reminder as we read Pope's poem. They might be occasionally suspended, but they were still there, and continued to exert a powerful influence on English criticism (particularly in drama) until the mid-eighteenth century and beyond.

Though he helped translate Boileau's Horatian *L'Art Poetique* (1683), Dryden's great body of criticism is in prose. Pope therefore had more immediate models for his *Essay*, in the form of verse essays composed by figures whom he respected and in some cases knew personally. A widely admired example of this genre was *An Essay on Translated Verse* (1684) by the Earl of Roscommon (who had translated Horace's *Ars Poetica* in 1680). Roscommon's revised ending to this poem is particularly interesting for its sudden switch out of heroic couplets into Miltonic blank verse (i.e. *un*rhymed iambic pentameters) as he moves from Horatian poise and judgement to an attempt to imitate the 'sublimity' of Milton's *Paradise Lost*. Roscommon's poem in fact awkwardly bestrides the two traditions, and he finds that to handle them he needs two entirely different kinds of verse. The poem stops at that point without resolving the strange mixture. Pope never falls into such a trap and it is noticeable how he is able to encompass contrasting elements in a consistent but flexible style. It is an achievement we should not take for granted.

Another model for Pope was a short poem by his early patron George Granville, later Baron Lansdowne (soon to be the dedicatee of *Windsor Forest*). Granville's *Essay upon Unnatural Flights in Poetry* (1701) is a rather halting effort. Its theme, however, has a bearing on Pope's *Essay*. Granville's poem contrasts the 'audacious flight' of poetry (seen as building castles in the air) with the enduring stability of Truth (building on rock). The only way to reach the skies, he concludes, is by constructing your work upon the solid foundations of Truth ('Firm and unshaken, till it touch the skies'). Embarrassment at the Longinus-like 'unnatural flights' of poetry leads him to recommend a structure that is awkwardly reminiscent of the Tower of Babel. Again we see a poet having some difficulty in reconciling the two traditions.

(ii) The Poem

Turning to *An Essay on Criticism* we discover that Pope is aware of having to find his way through various competing ideas. In fact, he ends the poem with a passage charting the history of criticism (643–728), and from these lines we can see that he recognizes both the positive and negative sides of the ancient Rules. He concedes that Greece and Rome supplied '*useful Laws*' (682) (a phrase which echoes the 'useful Rules' of line 92). Pope's stress therefore is on their usefulness and practicality – they are only to be valued for the help they can give. To reinforce this point he contrasts the servile neoclassicism of modern French critics with the greater independence of his own countrymen:

> But *Critic Learning* flourish'd most in *France*.
> The *Rules*, a Nation born to serve, obeys,
> And *Boileau* still in Right of *Horace* sways.
> But *we*, brave *Britons*, *Foreign Laws* despis'd,
> And kept *unconquer'd*, and *unciviliz'd*,

> Fierce for the *Liberties of Wit*, and bold,
> We still defy'd the *Romans*, as *of old*.
>
> (712–18)

The tone of this passage is complex: servility is wrong, but the libertarian spirit of the English (defending the freedom of their wit) comes across as rather stubborn and prejudiced. Others knew better on this issue, he says, and turns to compliment Roscommon's *Essay* and another text which influenced him, the *Essay on Poetry* (1682) by John Sheffield, Duke of Buckingham (whose works Pope edited after the author's death). In this poem, says Pope, Sheffield asserted 'the *juster Ancient Cause*', and '*restor'd* Wit's *Fundamental Laws*' (721–2). This suggests that Pope is distinguishing between laws which are fundamental and just (i.e. somehow natural and inherent) and the laws rigidly imposed by some modern frenchified critics – in other words, between Natural Law and mere legalism.

Pope certainly shows respect for both Horace *and* Longinus. He understands clearly the contrasting principles involved, but instead of using one as a stick to beat the other, he allows each critic his greatness and rejoices in their separate characters. This is his tribute to Horace, which beautifully catches the Roman poet's ease of manner and his ability to reconcile different elements:

> *Horace* still charms with graceful Negligence,
> And without Method *talks* us into Sense,
> Will like a *Friend* familiarly convey
> The *truest Notions* in the *easiest way*.
> He, who Supream in Judgment, as in Wit,
> Might boldly censure, as he boldly writ,
> Yet *judg'd* with *Coolness* tho' he sung with *Fire*;
> His *Precepts* teach but what his *Works* inspire.
>
> (653–60)

This is both an exact characterization and a fine tribute. But Pope also values the contrasting figure of Longinus. If Horace balances coolness and fire, then Longinus is bold and blazing – but an equally powerful example:

> Thee, bold *Longinus*! all the Nine inspire,
> And bless *their Critick* with a *Poet's Fire*.
> An ardent *Judge*, who Zealous in his Trust,
> With *Warmth* gives Sentence, yet is always *Just*;
> Whose *own Example* strengthens all his Laws,
> And *Is himself* that great *Sublime* he draws.
>
> (675–80)

From its opening exclamation this catches the Longinian manner, just as the previous passage had caught the Horatian. But Longinus too is judicious: his judgements about writing are both passionate *and* true. The rhyme of *Just* with *Trust* suggests the intuitive nature of such judgement compared with Horace's. Pope places Horace in a social setting with a friend, while Longinus occupies a more rarefied atmosphere as the darling of the nine Muses. And, importantly, each critic is praised for being true to himself: in either case the man's criticism is a product of his personal integrity.

This stress on the personal and human is something that we notice throughout *An Essay on Criticism.* Pope places both criticism and literature within a human context. Where 'Truth' for Granville and Roscommon had been a spiritless abstraction, Pope's 'Truth' is a moral imperative at the heart of all human relationships:

> 'Tis not enough, Taste, Judgment, Learning, join;
> In all you speak, let Truth and Candor shine:
> That not alone what to your *Sense* is due,
> All may allow; but seek your *Friendship* too.
>
> (562–5)

This is not metaphysical Truth, but a humane Candour, and the benefits of just criticism can extend to friendship (as they did in Pope's life).

The basic tool shared by poet and critic is the capacity for 'Judgment'. This is not just an ability to separate good from bad, but is the faculty of distinguishing between the elements of a work, understanding its context and appreciating the author's intentions. Pope's judgement, then, is not merely censorious, but is part of the creative process. The problem is that each individual 'believes his own' (10), just as he would his watch. Judgement, therefore, if it is to mean anything, needs to be founded on some general principle, and Pope finds this in the concept of 'Nature'. It is not just the nature of things as they are, but is a universal divine power:

> First follow NATURE, and your Judgment frame
> By her just Standard, which is still the same:
> *Unerring Nature*, still divinely bright,
> One *clear*, *unchang'd*, and *Universal* Light,
> Life, Force, and Beauty, must to all impart,
> At once the *Source*, and *End*, and *Test* of *Art*.
>
> (68–73)

An Essay on Criticism

The term 'Nature' is the most problematic word in eighteenth-century literature (see Pope's discussion of it in a different context, in the *Epistle to Burlington*, p. 93 below). It is not an external standard, but an inner living principle. We usually know what we mean when we praise something as being 'natural'. We might be saying that it is lifelike, looks or feels 'right', is the opposite of 'artificial' (a term that suggests stiffness or falseness), is sincere and unaffected, suitable, even good for us. If we also bear in mind the Horatian concept of Decorum and add to this bundle of ideas the notion of a powerful divine principle implanted in ourselves and all living things, then we shall be coming close to Pope's meaning. Applied to writing, it becomes for him the equivalent of the life-force itself:

> In some fair Body thus th'informing Soul
> With Spirits feeds, with Vigour fills the whole,
> Each Motion guides, and ev'ry Nerve sustains;
> *It self unseen*, but in th'*Effects*, remains.
>
> (76–9)

But as if he realizes that an *external* standard is also important, he reminds us that the great Virgil (*Maro*) did not merely draw 'from *Nature's Fountains*', but also from the example of Homer: '*Nature* and *Homer* were, he found, the *same*' (133,5). The principle of Nature is so embedded in the words of Homer and other ancient writers that 'To copy *Nature* is to copy *Them*' (140). Useful rules, therefore, which are founded on the practice of the ancients are valuable because they are not regulations, but laws of Nature:

> Those R U L E S of old *discover'd*, not *devis'd*,
> Are *Nature* still, but *Nature Methodiz'd*;
>
> (88–9)

After all, what is important is not whether the rules have been followed, but whether the desired result has been obtained ('if you must offend/Against the *Precept*, ne'er transgress its *End*', 163–4). With this in mind it is clear that technical 'offenders' may in fact succeed:

> If, where the *Rules* not far enough extend,
> (Since Rules were made but to promote their End)
> Some Lucky L I C E N C E answers to the full
> Th'Intent propos'd, *that Licence* is a *Rule*.
> Thus *Pegasus*, a nearer way to take,
> May boldly deviate from the common Track.

> Great Wits sometimes may *gloriously offend*,
> And *rise* to *Faults* true Criticks *dare not mend*;
> From *vulgar Bounds* with *brave Disorder* part,
> And *snatch* a *Grace* beyond the Reach of Art

(146–55)

Here, with the language of Longinian boldness, Pope considers how the boundaries may be crossed, and how Pegasus (the symbolic flying horse of poetic aspiration) may discover a short-cut and the poet's goal be reached 'without passing thro' the *Judgment*' (156). The success is risky and momentary (*Lucky, snatch*), but no less valuable. In the hands of a poetic genius such behaviour may be licentious, but also licensed.

In this passage Pope, where we might expect the word 'Genius' uses the term 'Wit'. This alerts us to the difficulties of this word which occurs so frequently throughout the *Essay*. We tend nowadays to confine the term 'Wit' to a sharp kind of humour, but this is only a small part of the meaning it had for Pope and his contemporaries. It could indeed at the highest level be the equivalent of 'Genius', since it was generally used for a quickness of mind or agility of imagination, particularly the ability to join ideas or images together in new combinations (as such it could be a strongly imaginative quality). It was creative, but unsteady and unpredictable, often momentary in its effect. At its best it is 'sprightly' (302) and genuinely creative, the essential element of poetic power, and it can even be used virtually as the equivalent of the word 'poetry' itself (as in lines 494, 508, or 727 where Pope speaks of 'the Wit of *Greece* and *Rome*'). Dryden had concluded that 'Great Wits are sure to Madness near ally'd' (*Absalom and Achitophel*, 1681, line 163), and wit's instability and unsteadiness could lead it astray. Pope's youthful experience of trying to prune the poet Wycherley's exuberant wit had taught him that, and he may have had his old friend in mind in the following lines about how wit can go wrong:

> Some to *Conceit* alone their Taste confine,
> And glitt'ring Thoughts struck out at ev'ry Line;
> Pleas'd with a Work where nothing's just or fit;
> One *glaring Chaos* and *wild Heap* of *Wit*

(289–92)

Here wit is reduced to mere glitter, where extravagant similes (*Conceit*) and oddly shaped ideas take over, with the images tumbling over each other and any sense of theme or structure lost. It is in this context that Pope makes one of his most famous (and misunderstood) statements:

> *True Wit* is *Nature* to Advantage drest,
> What oft was *Thought*, but ne'er so well *Exprest*,
> *Something*, whose Truth convinc'd at Sight we find,
> That gives us back the Image of our Mind
>
> (297–300)

It would be misleading to think Pope simply means that true wit is beautifully expressed commonplaces (and his statement to Spence that he had originally drafted out the ideas of *An Essay on Criticism* in prose might seem to support this). He is focusing here on wit's expressive aspect, recommending that it should not cover its subject with ornaments and jewels, but present it decorously in a garment of 'modest Plainness' (302) allowing the figure beneath to be seen (a woman in classical dress, perhaps, rather than swathed head-to-foot in corsets, frills and flounces). Nor is *What oft was Thought* mere 'commonplace' in our modern sense; we should remember that the word 'common' also means 'shared', and that Pope is looking for thoughts which find an echo in the reader's own experience, feelings and ideas that strike home to people's hearts as if they had always known them, but never till now understood them.

This is not as easy as it sounds. In fact one of the most notable features of *An Essay on Criticism* is its confrontation with difficulty. Pope's heroic-couplet recommendations never sink into being a handy recipe for success (we remember that Pegasus' short-cut was not the easier track). 'True Ease in Writing comes from Art, not Chance' (362), and some of the most memorable lines in the poem are those which convey the uncertainty, vulnerability and the sheer hard toil of poetry: the passage describing how the first exciting vision always fades away like the colours of the rainbow (488–93), or the lines about the career of the poet tackling the massive Alps of creative endeavour (220–32).

If poetry is difficult, then the critic should not shirk the labour and responsibility of his own calling. The bad critic, for Pope, lazily carries along all his own comfortable prejudices and indulges his natural vices and passions. For such a man, pride, spite and anger become substitutes for living thought (204, 31, 585). He never challenges himself with a fresh viewpoint or tries to discover the writer's aims:

> A perfect Judge will *read* each Work of Wit
> With the same Spirit that its Author *writ*
>
> (233–4)

This task involves examining the parts and assessing how they contribute to the whole effect; the critic must not pick out bits here and there to cavil at. He must recognize the '*Freer Beauties*' (170) and find the proper distance and proportion in which to view them. He must have knowledge, and if he cannot ideally be a writer himself (15–16), he should share a sense of the poet's task. If he is not sure of his ideas he should remain silent (566). The last thing he should be is merely servile, following the latest trendy ideas (409) or flattering influential people (420).

Pope's ideal, therefore, is not abstract perfection. Rather it is a fusion of those qualities we would look for in a friend as much as in a critic ('For each *Ill Author* is as bad a *Friend*' (519)). It is this consistently human scale against which Pope measures things that makes *An Essay on Criticism* such a refreshing and sane document:

> But where's the Man, who Counsel *can* bestow,
> Still *pleas'd* to *teach*, and yet not *proud* to *know*?
> Unbiass'd, or by *Favour* or by *Spite*;
> Not *dully prepossest*, nor *blindly right*;
> Tho' *Learn'd*, well-bred; and tho' well-bred, sincere;
> Modestly bold, and Humanly severe?
> Who to a *Friend* his Faults can freely show,
> And gladly praise the Merit of a *Foe*?
> Blest with a *Taste* exact, yet unconfin'd;
> A *Knowledge* both of *Books* and *Humankind*;
> Gen'rous Converse; a *Soul* exempt from *Pride*;
> And *Love to Praise*, with *Reason* on his Side?
>
> (631–42)

Those are the finest words ever written about the critic's task.

4. *Windsor Forest*

Windsor Forest is at the same time a nature poem and a political poem – or rather a nature poem that *grew into* a political one. Pope claimed to have written the original version of the first half (to line 290) when he was no more than sixteen years old, and the remainder was added for its publication in 1713. The completed poem was issued to celebrate the signing of the Peace of Utrecht, which brought to an end the long European war. The negotiations of the Tory government (with Bolingbroke playing a leading role) had been long and controversial, and Pope's praise of the Peace is making a clear party-political point. The poem was dedicated to George Granville, Lord Lansdowne, one of the twelve Tory peers created in 1711 to ensure government support in the House of Lords.

Pope's own notes make it clear that the earlier text was altered to fit its contemporary political context. For example, the original version of lines 235–6 was:

> Happy the man who to the shades retires,
> But doubly happy, if the Muse inspires!

which became in 1713:

> Happy the Man whom this bright Court approves,
> His Sov'reign favours, and his Country loves;
> Happy next him who to these Shades retires,
> Whom Nature charms, and whom the Muse inspires

Clearly the priorities have changed. The poet who was content to retire to the shades now sees fulfilment in terms of duty and patriotism. The happiness of fleeing from the Court now takes second place. Yet Pope deliberately keeps the phrase *Happy the man*, because for most eighteenth-century readers it would recall a very famous classical poem in praise of retirement, Horace's Ode *Beatus ille* ('Happy is the man'). It was an extremely influential text which can claim to have established a tradition of poetry praising rural retreat away from the Court and the places of business and power, asserting the values of a life of innocent contentment. Pope had himself written a version of this ode 'at about twelve years old' which began:

> Happy the man, whose wish and care
> A few paternal acres bound,
> Content to breathe his native air,
>   In his own ground.

(Ode on Solitude, 1–4)

In retaining the phrase *Happy the man*, therefore, but now placing it in the context of *Court*, *Sov'reign* and *Country*, Pope signals that his work moves the traditional poem of pastoral retreat towards a patriotic and political theme.

The term 'forest' may mislead us nowadays. In the Middle Ages up to Pope's day it did not mean a wood, but rather an area owned by the King and preserved by strict laws for royal hunting. Windsor Forest was therefore a considerably varied landscape under special protection and steeped in Royal associations. It links in Pope's mind his own family home at Binfield and the famous castle of Windsor itself. Just as important as the pastoral elements, therefore, are these patriotic, nostalgic and historical connections, and Pope fuses them into a poem which ranges through past, present and future, using landscape and its associations to make all kinds of points about human nature and human society.

No sooner has the poem begun than we appear to be back in the *Groves of Eden* (7), mankind's earliest landscape:

> Here Hills and Vales, the Woodland and the Plain,
> Here Earth and Water seem to strive again,
> Not *Chaos*-like together crush'd and bruis'd,
> But as the World, harmoniously confus'd:
> Where Order in Variety we see,
> And where, tho' all things differ, all agree.

(11–16)

At first sight these lines allude merely to the landscape of the forest (the *chequer'd Scene*, 17), but like many of Pope's descriptions this works on more than one level. If we re-read the lines we see that he begins to talk about the earth itself and the wider concept of 'Nature' – not just Nature in the sense of 'natural surroundings', but a principle in the world which includes the Nature of mankind. The notion of *Order in Variety*, for example, is as valid for the way we humans experience life as it is for a landscape, and it is a principle often seen at work artistically in Pope's poetry. Through the phrase *Order in Variety*, related here to the idea of being *harmoniously confus'd*, Pope gives his reader a way of thinking

42

about *Windsor Forest* itself. As a poem it can easily seem episodic and loose, but the more it is pondered the more its themes and incidents come together, so that a poem of great variety is seen to be beautifully and logically ordered. Its apparent confusion is in fact a subtle fusing together into a harmonious whole. Pope places the above passage towards the beginning of *Windsor Forest* to establish a principle which will help us to read and understand his poem.

Under the reign of Anne ('a STUART', 42) the fertile and well-cultivated forest seems to be alive with the gods of ancient Greece and Rome, those deities (Pan, Pomona, Flora and Ceres) who presided over various aspects of the fruitful natural world (its flocks, fruits, flowers and harvests). A link is established between the nation now looking forward to a period of 'Peace and Plenty' (42) under Queen Anne's Tory government, and the land once ruled by the gods on Mount Olympus (33). But at once Pope disrupts this peace and harmony by moving to the cruel forest-law in the wake of the Norman Conquest of 1066. Under William the Conqueror and his successor William II, says Pope, England was ruled by foreign tyrants, men who did not work *with* Nature, but were 'lonely Lords of empty Wilds and Woods' (48). As Pope develops this theme we understand his tactics: their alienation from, and misuse of, the forest is a sign of their denial of 'natural' human rights and feelings. Such despotism is *lonely* because it does not work with the people. The violation of nature expresses their violation of natural law ('The Fields are ravish'd', 65), and the barren landscape and ruined classical buildings symbolize the way such tyranny has broken the links with an old harmonious existence:

> The levell'd Towns with Weeds lie cover'd o'er,
> The hollow Winds thro' naked Temples roar;
> Round broken Columns clasping Ivy twin'd;
> O'er Heaps of Ruin stalk'd the stately Hind

(67–70)

The word *naked* shows that Pope is wishing to suggest human suffering also, and the single *stately Hind* roams the ruined scene like a noble remnant of a once-proud race, decimated but not yet exterminated. There is a satisfying irony when Pope goes on to describe the death of William II (accidentally shot in the forest) in terms of a dying animal:

> Lo *Rufus*, tugging at the deadly Dart,
> Bleeds in the Forest, like a wounded Hart.

(83–4)

Some of Pope's contemporary Roman Catholic readers would recall that another foreign tyrant called William (the Dutchman who became William III) cruelly persecuted his Catholic subjects and died in 1702 as a result of a fall while hunting.

After establishing a link between misuse of the forest and mistreatment of the kingdom, Pope describes the cruel field-sports of hunting, shooting and fishing (lines 93–164). We are not spared a sense of the pain of death. The pheasant, for instance, seems to offer a brief parable of the cruelty of fate, a brief pride before the fall:

> See! from the Brake the whirring Pheasant springs,
> And mounts exulting on triumphant Wings;
> Short is his Joy! he feels the fiery Wound,
> Flutters in Blood, and panting beats the Ground.
>
> (111–14)

His death is more than the death of a single bird. As the tone of pathos strikes us we see that Pope is conveying the impermanence of all living beauty; this exotic creature cannot be excepted from the fate appointed him:

> Ah! what avail his glossie, varying Dyes,
> His Purple Crest, and Scarlet-circled Eyes,
> The vivid Green his shining Plumes unfold;
> His painted Wings, and Breast that flames with Gold?
>
> (115–18)

As the destruction continues (the hare chased by the beagles; the doves, woodcocks, lapwings and larks shot by the fowler; the brightly coloured fish caught by the angler, and the hart relentlessly pursued by the hunter) all are sacrificed as part of the natural activity of the forest. The tone moves from pathos to fascination, to enthusiasm, and by the time Queen Anne enters the poem again at line 162 (now as a keen huntswoman) it is clear that this whole passage, while tinged with regret, is describing the proper use of the forest. This interpretation is reinforced later in the poem by lines 371–4, where Pope invokes the coming peace in terms which recall the earlier passage:

> The shady Empire shall retain no Trace
> Of War or Blood, but in the Sylvan Chace,
> The Trumpets sleep, while chearful Horns are blown,
> And Arms employ'd on Birds and Beasts alone.

The natural slaughter of the forest-sports is seen as exorcizing the wider violence. The trumpet blasts of war are transformed into the hunting-horn, the guns trained on animals rather than men. Whatever we may nowadays think of the organized killing of innocent creatures in 'sport', we can appreciate Pope's wider point. Nor is it a new idea: Ben Jonson in 1611 had celebrated the fruitfulness of an estate by describing how the birds and fish are 'willing to be killed' (*To Penshurst*, 30). In fact, the original note in Pope is the pathos with which he describes their deaths.

The theme of hunting not surprisingly calls to mind the classical figure of Diana the Huntress, goddess of the chase and of chastity. Pope's exorbitant assertion that Anne is 'as bright a Goddess, and as chast a Queen' (162) is a compliment to Anne's fidelity within marriage (what might be termed 'marital chastity'). This leads on to a passage (171–218) in which violation is presented in sexual terms. Pope concocts the story of Lodona, a nymph of Diana who is pursued by Pan, and at the moment of violation cries out to Diana (or Cynthia, her other name) and is magically metamorphosed into a stream. At the instant of trans-formation the metaphor (comparing Lodona's chastity to a pure, cool stream) comes alive, and she quite literally melts into tears:

> 'Let me, O let me, to the Shades repair,
> My native Shades – there weep, and murmur there.'
> She said, and melting as in Tears she lay,
> In a soft, silver Stream dissolv'd away.
> The silver Stream her Virgin Coldness keeps,
> For ever murmurs, and for ever weeps
>
> (201–6)

Pope places his repetitions skilfully (*Let me, O let me, Shades . . . Shades, there . . . there, silver Stream . . . silver Stream, for ever . . . for ever, weep, and murmur . . . murmurs, and . . . weeps*) in order to convey after the dramatic crisis a sense of continuance and continuity, the 'chast Current' (209) that still runs in the form of the River Loddon, a tributary entering the Thames near Binfield.

Just as the Loddon flows into the mighty Thames, so Pope's poem modulates from the world of threatened beauty to a grander and more public theme as he considers the 'wealthier Tribute' (224) that the Thames in turn pays to the ocean ('*Neptune*'s self', 223). The 'tow'ring Oaks' are seen as 'future Navies', and the Court of Windsor as a new Olympus. But just at the moment we expect Pope to widen his patriotic theme (235–6), patriotism immediately appears in a more private, introspective guise in the form of great men (Scipio and Atticus) who, like his friend

and patron Sir William Trumbull, withdrew from public life to 'humbler
Joys of home-felt Quiet' (239). By this withdrawal they freed their
thoughts into a sphere far wider than that of worldly affairs:

> T'observe a Mean, be to himself a Friend,
> To follow Nature, and regard his End.
> Or looks on Heav'n with more than mortal Eyes,
> Bids his free Soul expatiate in the Skies
>
> (251–4)

Pope's lines combine the notion of a Horatian middle way (*Mean*) guided
by an awareness of one's own nature, and an expansion of the inner life
into infinity. This combination of drawing inwards and expanding outwards is a typically Popean idea, one which became increasingly urgent
as he discovered the sources of power within his own inner life. The life
beyond mortal affairs (an inner kingdom as well as a national one) is
here established before he allows his poem to expand into the public and
political realm.

Pope's approach is not made directly, but in terms of the local poetic
tradition, of which his patron Granville is the latest representative (once
again the present is seen as a culmination of the past). The Muses, whom
he invokes in line 259, eventually lead him back to the world of contemporary national issues, and allow him to relate his own poem to a
literary tradition. The first two figures, Sir John Denham and Abraham
Cowley (lines 263–82), had both taken the Royalist side in the Civil
Wars (1642–9) and their poetry had spanned both war and peace.
Denham's famous poem *Cooper's Hill* is related in both form and content
to *Windsor Forest*. Like Pope's, Denham's verses celebrate Windsor and
its rich historical connections; he sees the Thames as 'the world's exchange', paying its tribute to the sea and reaching out towards the
Indies; and throughout the poem runs the theme of freedom versus
tyranny. By complimenting Denham so specifically Pope is declaring
that his own poem stands in direct succession to *Cooper's Hill*. He is in
no way striving for total originality, but on the contrary hopes to aug-
ment and enrich the meaning of his poem by reference to his famous
predecessor. After all, a major theme of *Windsor Forest* is tradition and
the continuity of values. Such values, Pope implies, are still 'current',
like the small tributary supplying the Thames, which in turn supplies the
world beyond. This ever-flowing current of values remains as valid for
Pope's age as it did in earliest times. The recurrent imagery of flowing
water in the poem therefore provides a powerful unifying theme.

Thoughts of the Earl of Surrey (the sixteenth-century soldier and poet, and another celebrator of Windsor) call to mind the old warriors and heroes of the place: figures like Edward III and his son the Black Prince, who won glorious battles overseas, and two kings (Henry VI and Edward IV) who contended with each other for the throne during those earlier Civil Wars, the 'Wars of the Roses', and who now rest near each other in St George's Chapel, Windsor:

> Here o'er the Martyr-King the Marble weeps,
> And fast beside him, once-fear'd *Edward* sleeps . . .
> The Grave unites; where ev'n the Great find Rest,
> And blended lie th' Oppressor and th' Opprest!
>
> (313–18)

We recall those earlier lines about *where, tho' all things differ, all agree* and begin to understand how that principle of harmonious confusion is running through the poem. Here the warlike Edward and saintly Henry rest side by side, equal in death and reconciled after their bitter struggle, a point which of course echoes Pope's primary theme of peace-after-war.

At this point Pope turns to more recent history, the Civil Wars, the Great Plague (1665) and Great Fire of London (1666), after which the new settlement of Queen Anne brings the triumphs of peace:

> She saw her Sons with purple Deaths expire,
> Her sacred Domes involv'd in rolling Fire,
> A dreadful Series of Intestine Wars,
> Inglorious Triumphs, and dishonest Scars.
> At length great ANNA said – Let Discord cease!
> She said, the World obey'd, and all was *Peace*!
>
> (323–8)

This does not quite capture the complexities of seventy years of British History. The divine *fiat* of the Queen is to reappear (as we shall see) in a hilariously diminished context during the card game in *The Rape of the Lock*. Here it rings out as a rather awkward heroic gesture. As the word '*Peace*!' reverberates, Old Father Thames not surprisingly stirs himself from the ooze and appears with his engraved urn, surrounded by many lesser rivers who are all individually characterized, once more showing the *Order in Variety* which is such a vital principle in this poem. The tributary streams swell the Thames with their urns, and as the mighty current flows onward all the themes of the poem seem to come together as it heads towards its climax. The River God turns his gaze on Windsor Castle, and the culminating passage is his invocation of Peace, a

47

celebration of the Tory settlement of the long European war. The Thames characterizes himself as a river of peace in contrast to other world rivers:

> Let *Volga*'s Banks with Iron Squadrons shine,
> And Groves of Lances glitter on the *Rhine*,
> Let barb'rous *Ganges* arm a servile Train;
> Be mine the Blessings of a peaceful Reign.
>
> (363–6)

Pope is always eager to visualize argumentative points like these, and often uses light-effects (as here) to bring an emblematic scene to life. It is the technique of a painter. Added to this is the ironic reference to the 'Groves of Lances' (364) which makes a neat contrast with the peaceful groves of Windsor Forest. On the banks of the Thames the newly built villas seem to grow like trees ('ascending *Villa*'s', 375) and 'Project long Shadows o'er the Chrystal Tyde' (376), contributing naturally to the scene. Rural nature is obviously becoming reconciled to progress and development, and as we follow the stream London and Westminster come into view, not as jarring contrasts to the pastoral scene, but harmoniously coexisting with it ('I see, I see where two fair Cities bend/Their ample Bow', 379–80). The climax of this idea arrives when Pope wittily visualizes the trees of the forest volunteering to become ships:

> Thy Trees, fair *Windsor*! now shall leave their Woods,
> And half thy Forests rush into my Floods,
> Bear *Britain*'s Thunder, and her Cross display,
> To the bright Regions of the rising Day;
> Tempt Icy Seas, where scarce the Waters roll,
> Where clearer Flames glow round the frozen Pole;
> Or under Southern Skies exalt their Sails,
> Led by new Stars, and born by spicy Gales!
>
> (385–92)

The effect is extraordinary as the very trees of Windsor sail off to the four corners of the earth, dispersing peace and plenty. The local has flowed into the international, the homely transformed into the exotic, and the Thames, from its quiet sources within the pastoral retreat, now confidently explores and colonizes the world. As it does so, Pope's own poem widens its views by launching into a prophecy of the future (reaching out not just geographically but also temporally) and shifting its tone to one of grand generality:

> The Time shall come, when free as Seas or Wind
> Unbounded *Thames* shall flow for all Mankind,
> Whole Nations enter with each swelling Tyde,
> And Seas but join the Regions they divide
>
> (397–400)

The prospect is one of a now-universalized harmony, which has grown with the poem from its opening to embrace all mankind and to promise them a peaceful future after endless wars. Conquest ceases, slavery is no more, and. as Pope sees 'the new World launch forth to seek the Old' (402) we begin to appreciate how time and space have daringly combined, and how Pope's use throughout the poem of *the Old* has been part of a wider quest for original moral and social values. The Roman 'Augusta' (London) is now the 'old' world, the classic to which the New World will aspire. Continuity of values and ideals is thus established across the centuries, with Britain mediating the values of the past to the new world of the future.

To read *Windsor Forest* is to see the youthful Pope writing with confidence and daring. The twenty-four-year-old was obviously staking his claim to be not just a critic of taste in the world of literature, but a public poet to be read and admired by the leaders of his country, someone who could speak, if not for the nation, at least for the Tory government. The calculatedly naive ending does nothing to dispel a sense of Pope's public ambitions. He may seem to be making a modest bow:

> My humble Muse, in unambitious Strains,
> Paints the green Forests and the flow'ry Plains . . .
> Ev'n I more sweetly pass my careless Days,
> Pleas'd in the silent Shade with empty Praise;
> Enough for me, that to the listning Swains
> First in these Fields I sung the Sylvan Strains.
>
> (427–34)

As the young poet draws back into his shady forest retreat, his readers would recognize that it was with words similar to these that the great Virgil modestly ended his *Georgics*, one of the great classics of Latin literature. Nor was it long before he was to establish himself, through the *Aeneid*, as the greatest Latin epic poet.

5. The Rape of the Lock

The origins of Pope's brilliant mock-epic, *The Rape of the Lock*, are in gossip and scandal inside a closely knit community. The incident at the centre of the poem (the beautiful young Belinda's humiliation by the Baron, who in public snips off a curl from her hair as a kind of love-trophy) apparently alludes to an embarrassing incident between the young Lord Petre and Miss Arabella Fermor, one which had grown from a trivial incident into an angry quarrel between two prominent local Catholic families. Pope was asked by his friend John Caryll to 'laugh them together again', and so we should not be surprised that part of the poem's message is to recommend 'good Humour' (v, 30).

The notion of a 'storm in a teacup' is a familiar one, and if we think about the literal meaning of that phrase we shall have a good idea of how Pope's imagination was stirred (pun intended) by the incident. At the centre of his poem is a sense of disparity: a raging storm trapped inside a brittle, perfect vessel. On one level this precarious teacup is Belinda herself, the 'painted Vessel' (ii, 47) who throughout the poem is compared with a china jar, flawless and beautiful, her chastity still intact. She is threatened with a 'fall' from grace and with the loss of her honour, which will crack the surface she presents to the world and reduce her value. On another level the teacup is Pope's own poem, a perfect minia-ture containing all the furious passions, fierce battles and moral conflicts of a great classical epic. Throughout the poem these passions, repressed inside Belinda and also compressed in the miniaturized epic structure of Pope's poem, threaten to break out and destroy the vessel that contains them. It is these possibilities which give excitement to the work and make *The Rape of the Lock* a fine example of how Pope's poetry works through tension and contradiction, how it explores the relationship be-tween order and energy. We must not be misled by the smoothly polished surface of the poem, or think that it is merely decorative and trivial. The *subject* of the poem may be trivial, but the forces working below the surface are disturbing and fascinating.

Like any good scandal, *The Rape of the Lock* tempts us to uncover the 'facts' and reconstruct the incidents. The world of gossip works on whispered suggestions and dark hints, and so does Pope's poem. The first critical procedure, therefore, is to try and reconstruct the story, and

50

to do this we have to interpret the clues Pope has given us. We may be factually wrong, but unless we respond to the gossipy side of *The Rape of the Lock* we shall have missed a vital part of its character.

(i) The Plot of the Poem

As the poem opens, Belinda the young court beauty is lying late in bed. After trying to summon her maidservant in the room below by hammering on the floor with her slipper and ringing her hand-bell, she relapses into day-dreaming, half asleep and half awake. Into her slumbering mind comes a vision of a handsome beau (literally the young man of her dreams). She hears him flatter her and reassure her that she is the centre of a world of ethereal beauty. But then there is a note of warning: 'Beware of all, but most beware of Man!' (i, 114). This chilly note is her moment of awakening, as her impatient lap-dog licks her and recalls her to the world of real men and the adventures of the day. At this moment too Pope hints at the gossipy background to his work:

> 'Twas then *Belinda*! if Report say true,
> Thy Eyes first open'd on a *Billet-doux*;
> *Wounds, Charms*, and *Ardors*, were no sooner read,
> But all the Vision vanish'd from thy Head.

(i, 117–20)

The poet addresses his heroine, wondering aloud about the love-letter (*Billet-doux*). We know that her eyes *first opened* in line 14, and now they open on a love-letter as her lap-dog nuzzles her. Perhaps it has been tied around his neck? She reads it impatiently and we have a glimpse of the kind of letter it is: *Wounds, Charms, Ardors*, the typical jargon of french gallantry, of popular sentimental romance. The italicized words echo through Pope's lines as they resound in Belinda's mind while she reads, and they have their desired effect. The real 'beau' who wrote them obviously knows how to capture a girl's heart. But we soon learn that his love-letter is only one of many. The scene shifts to her dressing-table and the note is propped up among the 'Puffs, Powders, Patches, Bibles, Billet-doux' (i, 138). As Belinda changes before our eyes into a newly created goddess, we realize that this paragon of divine beauty (the 'heav'nly Image' in her mirror) is a transformation of the lazy stay-abed girl of the poem's opening. She is clearly being made ready for some dangerous exploit in which Beauty will be her weapon ('Now awful Beauty puts on all its Arms', i, 139).

At the beginning of the second canto we see the chief source of her power: the two locks which hang tantalizingly over her neck. These curls have been created by the sylphs at i, 146 (see also ii, 97), and they have the power of trapping the hearts of every man she meets. Her beauty is clearly aggressive and intimately linked to the power of the sylphs over her, and over the young men who 'fall' for her. With the introduction of 'Th'Adventrous *Baron*' (ii, 29) a missing piece falls into place. We discover that this is in fact a flashback, and that the Baron has been up since before dawn ('ere *Phoebus* rose', ii, 35) to prepare for his adventure. He is obviously a connoisseur of gallantry and has been a successful player in the game of love. He is determined to meet the force of Belinda's beauty with tactics of his own ('Force' or 'Fraud'). He has a collection of French romances, and uses twelve huge volumes to build an altar. On top of this he lays out his collection of sentimental trinkets, and they are consumed by the fires of love (literally his 'ardour') in the shape of a burning billet-doux. This is a man with the experience and resource-fulness to counter Belinda and her guardian sylphs, and to win their pride and joy. Obviously the morning billet-doux was his first tactical move, calculated to surprise and delight her.

The scene switches back to Belinda, now gliding along the Thames by boat to Court. The music, sunlight and breeze play around her. Her companions on board think they hear the wind whispering in the sails, but *we* know it is the sylphs watching over their charge. We glimpse them in the hazy atmosphere of the afternoon sun striking the clouds and in the colours of her dress shifting its tints as it catches the light.

With Canto Three we are inside Hampton Court (where the Court has assembled), at the very centre of the world of tittle-tattle bred inside that little exclusive society:

> In various Talk th'instructive hours they past,
> Who gave the *Ball*, or paid the *Visit* last:
> One speaks the Glory of the *British Queen*,
> And one describes a charming *Indian Screen*;
> A third interprets Motions, Looks, and Eyes;
> At ev'ry Word a Reputation dies.

(iii, 11–16)

In this world, gestures and glances (*Motions, Looks, and Eyes*) are full of meaning. The slightest hint or suspicion is enough to destroy a reputation with the rapidity of the flick of a fan or the taking of a pinch of snuff. It is a world where decorative surfaces (*a charming Indian Screen*) compete in importance with Queen Anne herself. It is a Court which has lost its reason for existence, a place of formal appearances rather than the real thing.

Our eyes light on Belinda, seated at the card-table and embarked upon a game of ombre. As the battle on the 'Velvet Plain' takes a crucial turn we become aware that one of her opponents is the Baron (iii, 66). Could this be an assignation suggested in his billet-doux? In any case, he begins to take control and wins a most significant trick in his own game:

> The *Knave of Diamonds* tries his wily Arts,
> And wins (oh shameful Chance!) the *Queen of Hearts*.
> At this, the Blood the Virgin's Cheek forsook,
> A livid Paleness spreads o'er all her Look
>
> (iii, 87–90)

Again the details hint at a hidden plot. Belinda loses *the Queen of Hearts* thanks to the Baron's *Knave of Diamonds*. Has he given her a jewel or ring? Does she at this moment 'lose her heart' to him? She changes colour as the blood leaves her cheeks. The winning trick which follows appears to make the victory hers, but as the coffee is ritually ground, infused and poured, and the Baron relishes the delicious liquor, he ponders on a way to claim his beautiful trophy. The lady Clarissa draws out her scissors from their case and hands them to him. As the Baron reaches out towards her hair, Ariel is about to intervene when he sees 'An Earthly Lover lurking at her Heart' (iii, 144). She is in love, this time not with a beautiful vision or a mere whimsical fancy, but with an *Earthly Lover* who has lodged himself in her heart. The sylphs preside, we have been told, only over a girl who 'rejects Mankind' (i, 68), and so in confusion and amazement Ariel realizes his powerlessness and slips away. Things of air (fancies, whims, daydreams) are no more; something living and human has taken their place. The sylphs can do nothing and they leave her 'for ever and for ever!' (154) at the instant the lock is severed from her head.

The Baron exults in his triumph and Belinda screams in horror. At this climactic moment of the drama the poem's surface activity suddenly ceases, and we enter, with Canto Four, a dark, internal world. This is the territory of Belinda's 'secret Passions' (iv, 2), a place beneath her waking, conscious life which she has repressed. It is the world of her Spleen, imaged as a dark cave of half-formed and misshapen beings, and into it ventures Umbriel the Gnome, representative of those forces of prudery which strive to exclude love, beauty and openness of feeling. When we first meet the poem's mythological population of sylphs and gnomes (i, 59–66) we discover that they are spirits of dead women now infused into their constituent elements. The coquettes (flighty women of an airy temperament who play the flirt and flit from beau to beau without ever being entangled) evaporate into sylphs, while the prudes sink into the earth (the human flesh, where they are at home in the dark internal recesses of people, repressed, ready to do mischief and spoil the fun of others by arousing uncomfortable fears and neuroses). In the eighteenth century it was thought that the function of the spleen was to purge the body of dark, melancholy vapours. If it functioned badly these would ascend and cloud the brain, bringing a fit of the 'vapours' or 'the Spleen', a malady to which women were thought especially prone. When Umbriel returns to the surface after his interview with the goddess Spleen he carries her two gifts with him containing her products: a bag of cries and sobs, and a vial full of griefs and tears. Umbriel releases the bag (iv, 91) over the heads of Belinda and her friend Thalestris, into whose arms she has sunk. In other words, we witness an attack of the Spleen. Thalestris voices her horror at her friend's disgrace, and her pompous beau, Sir Plume, vainly demands that the Baron surrender his trophy. At this point Umbriel breaks the vial over Belinda (iv, 142), and she and her 'pitying Audience' (v, 1) dissolve into tears.

At this point, with the opening of the final canto, Clarissa (whose scissors committed the fateful deed) steps forward and tries to prevent the inevitable catastrophe by injecting a note of good humour and common sense. Belinda has moved from one extreme to another, from a coquette to a prude, from the control of the sylphs to the power of the gnomes, from being a flirtatious, girlish daydreamer to an angry, guilt-ridden killjoy, an old maid before her time. Belinda's fall has ignored a whole area of human experience in between, and it is this that Clarissa attempts to reclaim. She reminds her of the world of commitments and responsibilities which does not exist in daydream or nightmare, but engages with how people actually live. It is not an ideal world, and within it are old age and smallpox; hair turns grey, and maidens marry and rear children. It is a world where 'she who scorns a Man, must die a Maid' (v, 28) and there is more at stake than in the game of love. Some day the dancing and dressing-up will have to stop, and it is good for a woman to understand that good humour, good sense and a genuine, deeply held virtue can outlast beauty and adolescent fun. But the answer is not to withdraw into a prudish isolation which cherishes a negative and sterile 'virtue'. Clarissa's words, with their knowing worldliness, are the fruit of experience, and she urges Belinda to be true to her genuine feelings and not be obsessed with what appears to be a public outrage on her honour.

But the *beau monde* of the Court greets Clarissa's words with grim silence, and from this moment violent passions take over. Umbriel sits aloft on a 'sconce' (a wall-mounted candlestick with a mirror attached) applauding gleefully, and we know that prudery is rampant. Belinda's little society relapses into chaos as beaux and wits are routed, snuff flies and hairpins are wielded as weapons. Amid the confusion the celebrated lock disappears. The individual hairs have flown off in all directions and the 'lock' exists no more. As it scatters into its constituent parts it remains only a glorious memory. But at this point Pope rescues the image of the Lock, allowing it to represent both Belinda's beauty and his own poem. It is turned, through Pope's fanciful ending, into a comet, trailing its curling hair behind it, and the sylphs joyfully pursue it through the heavens. The dramatic action of the poem may have ended in chaos and destruction, but thanks to his own poem, Arabella Fermor's beauty will survive the ravages of time and remain for future ages. Perhaps in the end the *idea* does survive the thing itself, but only when created and justified by great art.

(ii) Mock-heroic

A narrative poem like this is so much more than its story, but we must remember that for neoclassical critics of Pope's day the plot (or 'fable') of an epic poem was the most important element: for them it was the foundation on which all the other elements rested. It is therefore right that we have made some effort to do justice to the plot of *The Rape of the Lock* (and it is surprising how many critics tend to ignore it).

But alongside the story of Belinda and her lock are two other narratives running parallel, both of an epic kind. First, what we might term Belinda's 'heroic' plot is the story of the downfall of a mighty warrior who is the darling of the gods. He decks himself in his glittering armour and issues out into the world of men like the sun god on a regal progress. After being victorious in knightly combat by leading his troops to an exciting tactical victory, and at the very height of his triumph, fate intervenes. His divine guardians can no longer protect him, and the laurels are snatched from him by trickery. The strict code of war is outraged, honour is besmirched, and in the general battle that follows all the rules of epic combat are forgotten and the old heroic society disintegrates. According to this reading, Belinda's lock functions as a type of holy grail, the divine sanction for knightly endeavour and the thing that supplies an ideal for an otherwise fragmented and faithless society.

The second plot we might term 'the Fall of Belinda'. Whereas the 'heroic' plot draws on the world of classical epic (Homer, Virgil and the Romance epics of the Renaissance) this plot re-enacts the story in Milton's *Paradise Lost* of Adam and Eve's disobedience, their eating of the forbidden fruit from the Tree of Knowledge, and their consequent expulsion from the Garden of Eden. Eve's 'fall' in particular was due to her pride (in thinking herself wise and aspiring to divinity) and her foolish adventurousness when she had been warned in a dream of what might happen. The plot of Belinda's 'fall' echoes Eve's. She too is both flattered and warned in a dream, and Ariel whispers at her ear just as Satan (disguised as a toad) had done to Eve in Milton's epic. Belinda gazes at the image of her own beauty in the mirror in the way Eve was held spellbound by her reflection in a pool in momentary self-adoration; and just as the innocence of Adam and Eve is watched over by millions of spiritual forms, so is Belinda's purity. When her fall comes, as with Eve's, they are powerless to intervene. The 'dire Event' (ii, 141) recalls the terms in which Milton speaks of the Fall in *Paradise Lost*, and though Pope humorously transforms the event into the fall of a piece of China ('Or when rich *China* Vessels, fal'n from high / In glittring Dust and painted Fragments lie!', iii, 159–60), it is equally fatal and irrevocable. Finally, in the same way that Milton raises the issue of the 'Fortunate Fall' (the possibility that a greater good will finally come of evil), so the 'resurrection' into eternal life of the lock holds a kind of divine reassurance granted to those who believe and have faith in a higher power.

We can see, therefore, that Pope has cleverly run alongside his contemporary social drama the outlines of two older plots from heroic and Christian epic. *The Rape of the Lock* inherits the themes of these great stories, and some of its incidents are the direct descendants of memorable moments in the epics of Homer, Virgil and Milton transposed into the eighteenth-century drawing-room. Nowadays we come across these as footnotes in editions of Pope, and so it might be illuminating to look at a couple of representative incidents of this kind in more detail, before we go on to consider some of the implications of mock-heroic writing as it affects our reading of *The Rape of the Lock*.

The battle for the lock is at its height, when the king of the gods himself gives the mortals a sign:

> Now *Jove* suspends his golden Scales in Air,
> Weighs the Men's Wits against the Lady's Hair;
> The doubtful Beam long nods from side to side;
> At length the Wits mount up, the Hairs subside.
>
> (v, 71–4)

Suddenly a higher power than the sylphs and gnomes has intervened to weigh the lock of hair in cosmic scales. This jump from the human level to the divine, from the struggles of men to the destiny decreed by the heavens, is a recurrent epic motif. In Homer's *Iliad* the killing of Hector by Achilles is foreshadowed when Zeus (the Greek version of Jove) lifts up his golden scales to weigh their destinies. Here is Pope's own translation of that vital moment:

> *Jove* lifts the golden Balances, that show
> The Fates of mortal Men, and things below:
> Here each contending Hero's Lot he tries,
> And weighs, with equal Hand, their Destinies.
> Low sinks the Scale surcharg'd with *Hector*'s Fate;
> Heavy with Death it sinks, and Hell receives the Weight.
>
> (*Iliad* xxii, 271–6)

A parallel incident occurs in Book Eight of the *Iliad* where Zeus attempts to cheer the Trojans and discourage the Greeks, and in the closing episode of Virgil's *Aeneid* the fates of Aeneas and Turnus are similarly weighed during their fight to the death.

In *Paradise Lost* God uses a pair of golden scales to prevent an unnecessary fight by showing Satan how pointless it would be to resist the divine will. But in Milton's Christian context the 'loser' rises (being weighed in the balance and found wanting):

> The eternal to prevent such horrid fray
> Hung forth in heaven his golden scales . . .
>   . . . in these he put two weights
> The sequel each of parting and of fight;
> The latter quick up flew, and kicked the beam
>
> (*Paradise Lost*, iv, 996–1004)

In *The Rape of the Lock* Pope adds a footnote referring the reader to Homer and Virgil, rather than to Milton; so his mock-heroic scales probably indicate that the lock's fate is doomed (though of course it finally does mount up to the skies). But the allusion also helps Pope to make a moral point: the appearance of the scales during the battle for the lock is a reminder of the vanity of human endeavour in the face of

57

fate. Even though this is a petty quarrel, the same principles apply as
had applied to the great Hector: human heroics are of little account
when measured against the power of the divine.

A second incident with a long poetic ancestry is the 'dire Event' itself:

> The Peer now spreads the glitt'ring *Forfex* wide,
> T'inclose the Lock; now joins it, to divide.
> Ev'n then, before the fatal Engine clos'd,
> A wretched *Sylph* too fondly interpos'd;
> Fate urg'd the Sheers, and cut the *Sylph* in twain,
> (But Airy Substance soon unites again)
> The meeting Points the sacred Hair dissever
> From the fair Head, for ever and for ever!
>
> (iii, 147–54)

Pope's own note to these lines refers the reader to Book Six of *Paradise
Lost*. Here, during the War in Heaven, Satan is wounded by the sword
of the Archangel Michael. It is a significant moment when the fallen
angel for the first time feels physical pain:

> then Satan first knew pain,
> And writhed him to and fro convolved; so sore
> The griding sword with discontinuous wound
> Passed through him, but the ethereal substance closed
> Not long divisible
>
> (*Paradise Lost*, vi, 327–31)

But Pope's scissors, as well as being a humorous version of an angelic
sword, also take us back to the Trojan War and the world of classical
epic. In Dryden's 1697 translation of the *Aeneid* the Trojan Horse (the
deception by which the Greeks were able to enter and destroy Troy) is
called *the fatal Engine*. Pope therefore cleverly draws a parallel between
the two incidents, suggesting as he does so that each is an act of treachery,
but perhaps also hinting at the gullibility of Belinda?

Yet there is more. Belinda is a victim of love, and the greatest tragic
lover in classical epic is Virgil's Dido, who, having been deserted by
Aeneas, stabs herself in despair. Out of pity at her agony Juno sends
down Iris, the Rainbow, from Heaven. She trails behind her, says Virgil,
'a thousand colours shifting in the sun', and to claim Dido's life she
symbolically cuts off a lock of her hair. This is Dryden's translation of
one of the most beautiful passages in Latin poetry:

> Downward the various Goddess took her Flight;
> And drew a thousand Colours from the Light:

> Then stood above the dying Lover's Head,
> And said, I thus devote thee to the Dead.
> This Off'ring to th'Infernal Gods I bear:
> Thus while she spoke, she cut the fatal Hair;
> The struggling Soul was loos'd, and Life dissolv'd in Air.
>
> (*Aeneid* iv, 700–705)

In this passage we glimpse an ancestor of the sylphs, and are given an epic context for the cutting of the *fatal Hair*.

We have, then, two incidents (the appearance of Jove's golden scales and the cutting of the lock) among many others, where Pope is consciously writing in the epic tradition, and while Virgil followed Homer, and Milton followed both, Pope follows all three, as though *The Rape of the Lock* is the culmination of an epic tradition stretching from classical Greece, via Virgil and Milton, to himself. This placing of his poem within a line of descent is characteristic of the mock-heroic enterprise, where the boudoir or drawing-room is the modern equivalent of the epic battlefield, and the 'mighty Contests' (i, 2) of the old heroic society are glimpsed through the 'trivial Things' of the present. The grand gestures and great actions of epic are amusingly scaled down, so that modern society finds itself presented as a parody-world, all its pride and ambition laughably pictured as petty and trivial. Such a descent finds an image within the poem in the passage describing the ancestry of Belinda's bodkin (v, 87–96), which over many years has undergone a series of transformations: from the chain of office of her great great grandfather, to a buckle, to a child's whistle, to a hair ornament (very much a descent from an object of male authority to one of female vanity). This genealogy mirrors the genealogy of Pope's poem, where the Trojan War, the founding of Rome, and the battle between Satan and Mankind, end up being represented across a card-table or a coffee-table.

In the light of these examples the effect of mock-heroic seems straightforward: Pope is satirizing contemporary upper-class society for being obsessed with trivia; things have got out of proportion, modern values are all wrong, and if we measure them against the great actions and emotions of the past we shall see life in its true perspective. This explanation is valid so far as it goes, but the effect of mock-heroic is more subtle than that.

Proportion, measure, and perspective are the words I have used here; in other words, mock-heroic works by setting up one figure/situation/term against another, so that we get both a sense of similarity *and* difference. It is too simple to say that we judge between them and conclude that because one is important the other is trivial. We hardly need *The Rape of the Lock* to tell us that playing cards and drinking coffee are trivial, nor Hector and Dido to show us that Belinda is over-reacting to her situation. No, if we are true to our responses we will realize that the mock-heroic process is more complex. Firstly, our judgement is challenged by the delight we take in the incongruity itself; secondly, the shifts in scale make us think about how we see and evaluate things; and thirdly, the surprising appositions cause us to look freshly and perhaps see unexpected links between situations and ideas. In other words, mock-heroic is the heroic couplet writ large.

The deeper we begin to think, the more subtle Pope's handling of mock-heroic appears. Perhaps the epic allusions and heroic language in the poem, rather than simply pointing to a disparity in values, show also how the values of the old heroic society reappear *in modern terms*? Perhaps the modern beau is just as proud of his decorated snuff-box as the warrior used to be of his helmet? Perhaps what the petticoat guards *is* the equivalent (for a young lady) of Aeneas' shield, and just as necessary? In order to convey the total horror felt by Belinda at the theft of her lock, perhaps the poet needs to invoke the moment when the apple snapped off from the Tree of Knowledge? Perhaps the subsequent metamorphosis in Belinda *is* as total and irrevocable as the change in Adam and Eve after their fall? The more we think about the question of 'values' within a social group, the less confident we may be of declaring certain ones more, and others less, valid.

Some of the most effective satirical lines in the poem raise just this issue:

> Whether the Nymph shall break *Diana*'s Law,
> Or some frail *China* Jar receive a Flaw,
> Or stain her Honour, or her new Brocade,
> Forget her Pray'rs, or miss a Masquerade,
> Or lose her Heart, or Necklace, at a Ball;
> Or whether Heav'n has doom'd that *Shock* must fall.

(ii, 105–10)

We can look at this in two different ways: Pope is exposing the muddled values of eighteenth-century upper-class society, where women lose their heart as casually as a necklace. For them a stain on their honour is of no more consequence than a stain on their dress. But shift the perspective slightly and things change. In this society perhaps an abstract stain on a woman's honour is as palpable as a stain on brocade (impossible to obliterate without ruining the garment, difficult and embarrassing to hide in public, enough to render its value worthless). We are made to consider how a stain on a woman's honour could be felt as something tangible.

At one level *The Rape of the Lock* does ridicule the coterie of court beaux and belles; but the excitements of the poetry, with its imaginative metamorphoses and shifts of perspective and scale, have a complex effect. This is often evident in the resourcefulness of the mock-heroic language itself. A representative example is the line: 'While *China*'s Earth receives the smoking Tyde' (iii, 110). This uses lofty and portentous language for something as trivial as pouring coffee. We laugh at the ingenious way the poet pompously describes the hot liquid filling the china cups. But shift the perspective, and the little ritual moment gains a new magic. The cup is probably literally '*China*'s Earth' (Chinese porcelain was being imported into Europe), but as we think of this, the scale expands into a sublime scene of some vast volcanic eruption, a 'smoking Tyde' overwhelming the land. An awesome storm in a teacup indeed, and a premonition of the elemental conflict that is to come a few moments later.

Pope's use of mock-heroic in *The Rape of the Lock*, therefore, on one level satirizes the distorted perspectives and muddled trivialities of Belinda's world. But it goes beyond this, and uses these distortions to create new forms. It employs shifts in perspective to make us challenge our standard views of things. The muddle becomes a creative fusion of images, the triviality is imbued with such verbal power that we find our category of the 'trivial' is challenged. Pope uses mock-heroic not just as the weapon of a satirist, but for creative purposes.

The word 'trivial' is frequently used by critics about the poem. Those who dislike it find it trivial in itself; some who admire it see it as a satire on triviality. Perhaps to this we can add a third possibility: that the poem makes us less certain about what we categorize as trivial and important. The poem plays many tricks with perspective, as the comic play of size and scale have their effect. At one moment Ariel is a mighty general addressing his troops (ii, 73), the next he is an invisible spirit hiding on the nosegay in Belinda's breast. The adventures in the Cave of Spleen with its subterranean domed palace and windy grottoes is occurring, we must remember, inside Belinda herself. Just as this neurotic inner world is *expanded* into a weird landscape, so the external world can become *miniaturized*.

This happens with Belinda's dressing-table, where the whole world seems to have contracted into a few jars and trinkets:

> This Casket *India*'s glowing Gems unlocks,
> And all *Arabia* breathes from yonder Box.
> The Tortoise here and Elephant unite,
> Transform'd to *Combs*, the speckled and the white

(i, 133–6)

We are back with the storm in a teacup. Just as the 'vessel' of Belinda contains a vaporous inner world of the Spleen, so the box of perfumes traps 'all *Arabia*' inside itself. Whereas the gnomes enjoy releasing imprisoned vapours (as in Umbriel's troublemaking) the sylphs' aim is to keep the lid on such containers ('Nor let th'imprison'd Essences exhale', ii, 94).

According to ancient Indian mythology, the weight of the Earth was supported by an elephant, and the elephant in turn was supported by a tortoise. When asked what supported the tortoise, the Indian would reply 'something, he knew not what'. This story was told by the philosopher John Locke in his *Essay Concerning Human Understanding* (1690), and Pope would certainly have read it there. What his lines momentarily give us, therefore, is a miniaturized world-myth. Of course the tortoise-shell and ivory combs materially *are* the tortoise and elephant carved into the implements of a young lady's vanity. Yet with his witty allusion to the Hindu myth of the nature of the World, Pope stretches the scale of the image so that it reaches out instantaneously to the cosmic. In turn, the phrase '*Cosmetic* Pow'rs' (i, 124) brilliantly compresses it.

(iii) Belinda and the Sylphs

In such ways *The Rape of the Lock* simultaneously expands and compresses, and as it does so, our sense of fixed values is challenged. The perspective changes so rapidly that we are denied firm structures within which we can make a confident moral judgement. The complicating factor is beauty and how we respond to it. In face of Belinda's beauty, the poet himself speaks as an indulgent admirer:

> If to her share some Female Errors fall,
> Look on her Face, and you'll forget 'em all.

(ii, 17–18)

In revising an earlier version of the poem, Pope emended his original word *forgive* to read *forget* (line 18). The change is significant: to *forgive* relied on the language of morality for its meaning, whereas to *forget* temporarily suspends moral issues altogether. The distinction here is between *im*morality and *a*morality: the *im*moral transgresses ethical boundaries, the *a*moral eludes them.

In extending *The Rape of the Lock* from an earlier two-canto text (1712) to the five cantos of 1714, Pope introduced the machinery of the sylphs to preside over his heroine. These spirits evade human boundaries (physical, moral, legal or sexual):

> For Spirits, freed from mortal Laws, with ease
> Assume what Sexes and what Shapes they please.
>
> (i, 69–70)

The sylphs' allegiance to Belinda draws her into their world of dis-embodied beauty. The sylphs are her charisma, the soft focus through which she is seen. They enhance her charms by playing around her as a waft of her perfume, the glitter from her earrings, the rustle of her dress, the subtle shades of her complexion, above all as the intriguing curl of the lock across her neck. The sylphs exist as the intangible element in life, the added ingredient that transforms the mundane to the 'divine!':

> Some, Orb in Orb, around the Nymph extend,
> Some thrid the mazy Ringlets of her Hair,
> Some hang upon the Pendants of her Ear
>
> (ii, 138–140)

The sylphs also express Belinda's whimsicality: they work busily inside her emotions and imagination, ensuring that nothing takes her fancy for long:

> With varying Vanities, from ev'ry Part,
> They shift the moving Toyshop of their Heart;
> Where Wigs with Wigs, with Sword-knots Sword-knots strive,
> Beaus banish Beaus, and Coaches Coaches drive.
> This erring Mortals Levity may call,
> Oh blind to Truth! the *Sylphs* contrive it all.
>
> (i, 99–104)

Note how they resist the moral word *Levity*. Such disapproving labels belong among the *mortal Laws* from which the sylphs are free. This passage catches the way Belinda's fancy restlessly switches allegiance. There is no commitment, no integrity within her. An eighteenth-century *Toyshop* was what we nowadays call a 'fancy-goods shop', selling snuff-boxes, ribbons, scissors, fans, tortoiseshell combs, cane-handles, hair ornaments (in other words, all the fripperies that fill Belinda's world), and that is what Belinda's inner life has become.

*fashion-
able
world
society*

The sylphs of course express perfectly the value-system of the *beau monde*. What is important to both of them is what is on show. The precious china vessel, a collector's item, retains its value only so long as its surface remains unblemished. (What it contains is not the sylphs', or society's, concern.) Playing about the surfaces of things, the sylphs literally represent the superficiality of the social world, and under their influence the language of morality is transformed to the language of beauty. For them, a stain on their girl's honour and a stain on her brocade belong in the same category, and to protect her powder 'from too rude a Gale' (ii, 93) is as important as preserving her innocence (and the word *rude* suggests as much).

It is in this context that we should view Belinda's 'honour'. She is susceptible and fancy-free, and thanks to the sylphs this coquettishness has so far preserved her. Under their prompting, she plays the game of flirtation but never remains committed long enough to lose her virginity:

> What guards the Purity of melting Maids,
> In Courtly Balls and Midnight Masquerades,
> Safe from the treach'rous Friend, the daring Spark,
> The Glance by Day, the Whisper in the Dark;
> When kind Occasion prompts their warm Desires,
> When Musick softens, and when Dancing fires?
> 'Tis but their *Sylph*, the wise Celestials know,
> Tho' *Honour* is the Word with Men below.

(i, 71–8)

Spark, fires, warm, softens, melting: the imagery is of woman as a piece of wax. In the heat of passion she becomes pliable, impressionable, and loses hold on her identity. It is a dangerous world, and Belinda can only survive by submitting to the flux and being footloose and playful. Once again humanity's moral terminology (this time *Honour*) loses its force because it cannot cope with the fluid sylph-world into which Belinda is drawn. Her supposed *Honour* is not the result of any principle or choice (and therefore deserving the name 'moral'), but simply the happy result of the sylphs' conspiracy to keep her fancy on the move.

The effect of the sylphs on the poem is so great that they seem to determine its whole character, and it is true that the essence of *The Rape of the Lock* lies in those elements that the sylphs encourage: surface detail, fluidity, miniaturization, amoral elusiveness and intangible beauty. However, just in case we mistake their world for the real everyday world in which we all live, Pope for a moment opens a door so that we glimpse a very different scene beyond:

Mean while declining from the Noon of Day,
The Sun obliquely shoots his burning Ray;
The hungry Judges soon the Sentence sign,
And Wretches hang that Jury-men may Dine;
The Merchant from th'*Exchange* returns in Peace,
And the long Labours of the *Toilette* cease

(iii, 19–24)

The lines return us to the boudoir, but the door has remained ajar just long enough for us to catch sight of a world of harsh *judgment*. It is all Pope needs to remind us that there is another world, not far away, in which real decisions have to be made. It is against this chilly draught of reality that the sylphs defend 'th'imprison'd Essences' of the poem. They are indulgent, forgiving, and in their own terms innocent, and they would like everything else to be. But Clarissa too has seen that life cannot forever be insulated from reality, and her speech in Canto Five recalls at that crucial moment the world of hunger and hanging.

Where, then, does Pope stand on this? How far does he indulge his heroine, and how far does he judge her? Is he at the same time disapproving of her triviality and in love with her beauty? These are questions that readers of the poem must decide for themselves. But whatever conclusions we come to, we can be sure that Pope understands the complexity of issues like these. Perhaps in *The Rape of the Lock* he has given us an intricate world in which indulgence and judgement, beauty and truth, imagination and reality are made to engage one with another. Why should we force him to make a judgement for us?

6. *Elegy to the Memory of an Unfortunate Lady*

This brief 82-line *Elegy* became one of Pope's most popular and admired poems, particularly at the turn of the nineteenth century during the so-called 'Romantic' period, when Pope's reputation was under attack. It may at first sight appear simple enough in its language and theme, but the more it is read and pondered, the more questions and contradictions arise. The problem which first occurs is: who is speaking the poem? The 'poet' is obviously emotionally involved with the lady. We see him at the beginning in some kind of dramatic scene, confronted by her ghost which beckons him towards a glade in the woods. Her breast is bleeding and the sword she holds suggests the tragic story of a lover's suicide ('To act a Lover's or a *Roman*'s part?', 8). It is as if she had some message to deliver (like the ghost in *Hamlet*), but she disappears from view, and all we have seen is the silent gesture. We are not told whether the poet follows or attempts to question her, and so this opening promise of some kind of dramatized exchange is not carried through.

Instead the poet himself begins to conjecture about the fate of her soul (11–28). There is nothing in this specific to her own situation, and it appears strange that the poet sees her as a figure of ambition and aspiration ('The glorious fault of Angels and of Gods', 14), alluding to Satan the rebel angel cast down into Hell for aspiring to godhead. To interpret this as a 'glorious fault' is a piece of special pleading and ignores the fate of eternal damnation that awaited him. The poet sees the lady as heroic, daring to release her soul from its bodily prison before the appointed time:

> Most souls, 'tis true, but peep out once an age,
> Dull sullen pris'ners in the body's cage:
> Dim lights of life that burn a length of years,
> Useless, unseen, as lamps in sepulchres

(17–20)

But for a heroic figure freed from earthly shackles, the lady is oddly dumb and suffering. And if her soul was transported to heaven ('As into air the purer spirits flow,/ And sep'rate from their kindred dregs below', 25–6), why is she restlessly roaming the earth?

The enigma is increased when the poet immediately turns his anger

66

against the lady's family (29–46), particularly her uncle and guardian, and we are reminded of the dramatic implications of the opening. The passage develops into a fierce curse, which imagines the man's family suffering a spate of bereavements ('frequent herses shall besiege your gates', 38). This is oddly specific in its spite and is said with a kind of relish, a tone which is highlighted when there follows a sudden shift to a contrasting language of dignified impersonality:

> Thus unlamented pass the proud away,
> The gaze of fools, and pageant of a day!
>
> (43–4)

It is strange how the poem moves between the language of urgent emotion and that of dignified elegy.

In the next paragraph (47–68) the poet turns to address the lady ('oh ever-injur'd shade!'), but the dramatic stance has gone. There is no sense that the lady hears or responds to him. The theme now is the loneliness and isolation of her death, and as the poet drives this home the language takes on the qualities of a dirge, its mournful repeated phrases tolling like a funeral bell:

> By foreign hands thy dying eyes were clos'd,
> By foreign hands thy decent limbs compos'd,
> By foreign hands thy humble grave adorn'd,
> By strangers honour'd, and by strangers mourn'd!
>
> (51–4)

It is as though she were being interred anew by the poet himself as he imagines the scene and gradually withdraws his eyes from her body, to her grave, to the mourners. He mutters at line 64 a version of the traditional Roman epitaph (let the earth lie lightly on you), awards the grave a few silver-winged angels, and finally consecrates it. The poet, in other words, is not here describing a scene, but is using his own language to create it, in this case to perform the holy rites and sanctify her resting-place.

His own formal epitaph follows (69–74), and again the tone shifts. All obsequies now are unavailing. At one stroke his loving and comforting words are shown to have no meaning in the face of death, which levels all (indeed equalizes the lady and her cruel uncle) and presents us with the single reality of mortal ashes:

> So peaceful rests, without a stone, a name,
> What once had beauty, titles, wealth, and fame.

> How lov'd, how honour'd once, avails thee not,
> To whom related, or by whom begot;
> A heap of dust alone remains of thee;
> 'Tis all thou art, and all the proud shall be!

Here everything (illusions and comforts) is stripped away, and we realize that from the beginning the poet has refused to reconstruct her as she was in life. Her 'beauty, titles, wealth, and fame' remain unknown to us as the poem ends. 'To whom related, or by whom begot' is a question the poet has decided not to answer. Even the 'name' has been missing throughout. The poet cannot give her a stone, and all that she has (in fact the only thing that keeps her in contact with us as readers) is the poet's memory, the fact that she lives within his heart and mind. But in the final paragraph of the poem (75–82) even this last connection is broken as the poet places himself in the same context of mortality as the lady. Both the singer and the subject of the song will die:

> Poets themselves must fall, like those they sung;
> Deaf the prais'd ear, and mute the tuneful tongue.
>
> (75–6)

The tongue and the ear are equally mortal, and the lines reach out to us readers also.

The two-sided attitude which the poet has taken towards mortal life is confirmed by the final lines, where he contemplates his own death. On one level this means a tragic parting from his beloved, but on another it is merely calling an end to the emptiness of life:

> Then from his closing eyes thy form shall part,
> And the last pang shall tear thee from his heart,
> Life's idle business at one gasp be o'er,
> The Muse forgot, and thou belov'd no more!
>
> (79–82)

The remarkable shift between lines 80 and 81 is at the heart of this poem's character. The attitude swings from what we can call the 'sentimental' to the 'stoic', in other words, from a position where his love is powerfully emotive to one where it can be soberly dismissed as just part of the empty ('idle') business of life. The *sentimentalist* (in the eighteenth-century sense) believes that feelings both have a value in themselves and also confer value on what is loved; whereas the *stoic* resists the ebb and flow of passion as being self-deluding. In this way the two positions are starkly opposed, and as we watch the poet alternating between the two

68

during the course of the *Elegy* we begin to see that he is working out ideas which go beyond a specific situation or the story of a 'real' person.

It is interesting to speculate biographically about how far Pope himself can be identified with the speaker of the poem, about what specific persons or situations may have been in his mind as he wrote it. This is intriguing, but finally unprofitable. What does come across, however, is that the poet-speaker is torn between two attitudes and between two kinds of poetry. Whether we call these sentimental and stoic, personal and impersonal, subjective and objective, or passionate and dispassionate, there is clearly throughout the *Elegy* a tension between these two kinds, and perhaps this is where we should locate the drama of the poem – within the poet himself. As we read more of Pope's work we may see him exploiting these two strains, rather less awkwardly than he does here, but with a similar feeling that the drama of a poem can exist not just in the story being told, but within the consciousness of the speaker. This awareness is particularly strong in another poem written at about this time, *Eloisa to Abelard*, which exploits such tensions to the full, and finds a speaker within whom a powerful drama can be concentrated.

7. *Eloisa to Abelard*

Eloisa to Abelard is unique among the poems we are discussing, because the poet speaks throughout in the voice of another character. 'Character', however, is a misleading word here (it suggests that Pope is writing a novel or a play and is attempting to create a consistent, fully rounded personality). Emphasis should perhaps be put instead on the idea of 'voice'. What we are given in the poem is a voice: frantic, despairing, pleading, loving, ecstatic, exhausted, and speaking by turns words of guilt or self-pity, of determination or lofty calm. A helpful exercise is to declaim part of it aloud and to gauge the various dramatic shifts in tone and volume. Such a reading would also convey the rhetorical power of the heroic couplets, which impose their own kind of formal discipline on her passion.

In the eighteenth century *Eloisa to Abelard* would have been recognized as a 'Heroic Epistle', a genre established by the Roman poet Ovid in his *Heroides*, which were a series of imaginary verse-letters written from one well-known figure to another under the pressure of some strong emotion. These were much imitated by Elizabethan and later poets, and the skill lay in charting the movements of feeling within the 'speaking' voice (which, being in letter-form, cannot be answered) and in conveying a sense of the person being addressed and of the past situation which has given rise to the letter. Because the letter is 'one way', the Heroic Epistle tends to specialize in frustration and self-justification.

The story of the lovers Eloisa and Abelard provided Pope with very suitable material for such an epistle. It was a famous tragic story, the incidents of which would be familiar to many of his readers (there were English and French 'editions' of their supposed letters). Abelard was one of the greatest scholars and theologians of the twelfth century, and the young Eloisa was his pupil, then lover, then secret wife. Her furious family took revenge in the crudest and most appropriate way by having Abelard forcibly castrated by ruffians. Eloisa ended as a Benedictine nun and abbess of a monastic house, the Paraclete, which he had founded. Years later a letter of Abelard's telling a friend about his misfortunes fell into her hands, and with it all her old feelings were aroused. In Pope's poem she writes to him from her bare cell in the Paraclete, alternately in despair, hope, frustration and ecstasy, yet knowing in her heart that her passion can never be consummated.

The poem has two landscapes: the physical surroundings of the convent, and the landscape of Eloisa's imagination which she projects on to its walls. Once again, we notice, Pope is fascinated by the containment of passion within an enclosed space. In *The Rape of the Lock* he took us into the dark cave inside Belinda and explored the shapes which haunted it. In *Eloisa to Abelard* the heroine herself is enclosed by the bare monastery walls:

> Relentless walls! whose darksom round contains
> Repentant sighs, and voluntary pains
>
> (17–18)

The walls are *relentless* because they are unyielding and cannot be moved by pity. They *contain* her sighs in the literal sense, but also they force her to *contain* her feelings within herself. She is surrounded by stone, and ironically it is a material on which human devotion has left its mark ('rugged rocks! which holy knees have worn', 19). She gazes on the statues, those 'pitying saints, whose statues learn to weep!' (22). But in spite of these images, Eloisa recognizes that stone cannot feel passion, unlike herself:

> Tho' cold like you, unmov'd, and silent grown,
> I have not yet forgot my self to stone.
>
> (23–4)

Against the ebb and flow of her passion these images of containment, calm and fixity seem to admonish her. She brings into this landscape the pulsing of human blood: the 'tumult' in her veins (4), the 'stubborn pulse' of her heart (27), and above all, the rapid flux of her imagination. Rising beyond these is the stony calm of Abelard himself, who has become in a strange way like the *unmov'd* statues:

> For thee the fates, severely kind, ordain
> A cool suspense from pleasure and from pain;
> Thy life a long, dead calm of fix'd repose;
> No pulse that riots, and no blood that glows.
>
> (249–52)

These contrasts between the fluid and the static, warmth and coolness, the passionate lover and the calm saint, run through the whole poem and contribute to the dramatic dilemma: 'Ev'n thou art cold – yet Eloisa loves' (260).

But there is also the Abelard of her memory continually exerting his presence. She recalls encountering his 'flame' (59), and how her imagination took him to be a shining angel ('My fancy form'd thee of Angelick kind', 61); how her feelings soon ran 'back thro' the paths of pleasing sense' (69) as the man took the angel's place. But now another image rises up before her:

> Alas how chang'd! what sudden horrors rise!
> A naked Lover bound and bleeding lies!
>
> (99–100)

This is one of several moments in the poem when Abelard becomes merged into the figure of Christ. Here her vision of him suggests the crucified lord. Her reference to 'the Maker' in line 140 is to Abelard as the founder of the convent as much as to God, and she confesses at the beginning that in her heart 'mix'd with God's, his lov'd Idea lies' (12).

This brings us to the central dilemma of the poem. As an enclosed nun, Eloisa chose the life of 'heav'nly-pensive' contemplation (2), a procedure that involved directing the imagination, and focusing the passions, upon images of Christ crucified and the bliss of the saints in Heaven. The purpose of such contemplation was to set aside the concerns of the flesh and to release the spirit in the hope of achieving, at the highest level, an ecstatic sense of union with God. The irony of Eloisa's situation is clear. She achieves a visionary soul-release, but in contrast to the 'golden dreams' of the virgin (216) hers brings only physical frustration:

> Then conscience sleeps, and leaving nature free,
> All my loose soul unbounded springs to thee ...
> Provoking Daemons all restraint remove,
> And stir within me ev'ry source of love.
> I hear thee, view thee, gaze o'er all thy charms,
> And round thy phantom glue my clasping arms.
>
> (227–34)

Instead of the saints there are *Provoking Daemons*; in place of the Holy Ghost there is the *phantom* of her lover; and her soul is not so much 'free' as *loose*, a word with overtones of immorality. In this way her visions imitate the formal meditative procedures of the contemplative life, but transpose all the terms into the language of human, rather than divine love. The 'spouse of God' fuses into the wife of Abelard, and a line like 'And swelling organs lift the rising soul' (272) develops a disturbing physicality at the ecstatic climax of the poem.

For centuries it has been recognized that religious ecstasy must express itself through the language of physical desire and consummation. The erotic *Song of Songs* in the Old Testament was thought to voice the love between Christ and the human soul, and Bernini's famous sculpture of 'The Ecstasy of St Teresa' visualizes her holy rapture as a piercingly sensuous moment. Eloisa's dilemma lies in the way she is forced to polarize these spiritual and physical levels of the meditative experience and set one against the other. Her contemplative training has given her the procedure and the terminology of ecstatic soul-release (this is really tautology, since 'ecstasy' literally meant the release of the soul from the flesh), but the image of Abelard has burst in and taken her over, turning her solitary meditation into a battleground between soul and flesh.

In her mind Eloisa tries to prise apart those images that have merged, to set Abelard *against* God, sometimes even with a sense that either alternative is equally preferable, just so long as one image completely drives out the other:

> Come, if thou dar'st, all charming as thou art!
> Oppose thy self to heav'n; dispute my heart;
> Come, with one glance of those deluding eyes,
> Blot out each bright Idea of the skies . . .
> Snatch me, just mounting, from the blest abode,
> Assist the Fiends and tear me from my God!
> No, fly me, fly me! far as Pole from Pole;
> Rise *Alps* between us! and whole oceans roll!
>
> (281–90)

This is in a literal sense polarizing what in her view have become the Sacred and the Profane. Confronted with an intense, unified emotional experience, she rives apart the terms of it and sets them in total opposition. She speaks at times like those heroines of French classical tragedy by Corneille or Racine who are torn between love and duty (lines 177–206). But this is a misleading parallel, in the sense that honour and duty, or any kind of social pressure, are not crucial to Eloisa, who instead inhabits a world of spiritual struggle (the Renaissance term 'Psychomachia') and remains close, even in her most despairing moments, to the standard contemplative procedures.

Eloisa's picturing of her own death (303–36) is another recommended meditative exercise, but again it offers itself to her in two contrasting forms. One (the voice from the shrine, 309–16) presents it as slipping away to a place of 'calm' and 'eternal sleep' (313), an image of easeful release which attracts her. But as she cries 'I come, I come!' the figure of Abelard reappears to make the moment of death one of ecstasy:

> Thou, *Abelard*! the last sad office pay,
> And smooth my passage to the realms of day:
> See my lips tremble, and my eye-balls roll,
> Suck my last breath, and catch my flying soul!
>
> (321–4)

After this climax, much depends on how we interpret the sudden 'Ah no' of the following line 325. It can be taken as Eloisa finally banishing her vision of the lover and substituting a priestlike Abelard 'in sacred vestments' holding the cross before her face. But even then, her imagined final moments are given a sweet languishing lovesickness, in that Abelard is made to watch the 'transient roses' fly from her cheeks and 'the last sparkle languish in my eye' (332). She wishes to die with Abelard hovering over her as the grieving lover.

Throughout the poem Eloisa is reaching out for sympathy (in its original sense of 'shared feeling'), and in a final neat twist (359–66) a 'sympathetic' link is made with her mediator, the poet himself, who has been voicing her 'well-sung woes'. With this sleight of hand Pope adds an extra emotive layer to the poem by introducing his own feelings for the Blount sisters, and particularly for Lady Mary Wortley Montagu whom he is 'condemn'd whole years in absence to deplore' (361). In the face of such mutual sympathy between the poet and the voice of the poem, it becomes difficult to judge Eloisa. Is she self-deceiving? Does she achieve some kind of transcendence of her situation? Is her Heaven merely a place of escape?

Because Pope's independent authorial voice is missing it is natural for us to supply our own judgement on Eloisa's spiritual status in terms such as these. We must be careful, however, to differentiate this from our assessment of the poem itself (which some critics do not). Part of the letter's power lies simply in the way it projects Eloisa's own voice to us, forcing us to feel the 'motion, pulse, and breath' (333) of her vexed meditation. Unique in Pope's output, *Eloisa to Abelard* is valuable in the way it isolates the pulse of passion that beats underneath so much of his poetry.

8. *An Essay on Man*

In the eighteenth century Pope's *Essay on Man* was his most widely read and admired work, and it established him as a writer of European fame. It has been calculated that during the hundred years or so following its publication in 1733–4 the poem was translated into Czech, Danish, Dutch (six times), French (sixteen times), German (about twenty-four times), Hungarian (twice), Icelandic, Italian (about eighteen times), Latin (five times), Polish (five times), Portuguese (twice), Rumanian, Russian (four times), Spanish (three times), Swedish (four times), Turkish, and Welsh (twice). These remarkable figures (taken from Maynard Mack's superb Twickenham edition of the poem) give us some idea of its universal appeal. Pope's subject, after all, is the nature of Man* and his place in creation; and in a mere thirteen hundred lines we are given a definitive statement about God's perfect design for the world, the scope of all living things, the role of mankind within the vast functioning system, and the implications this has for a person's conduct of his own life.

But *An Essay on Man* is also a poem of contrasts and contradictions – it does not simply versify a single system of thought. On the contrary it should rather be seen as placing competing systems side by side and playing one off against the other. The ideas that Pope reworks in the course of the poem have a long and complicated history, and its argument is sometimes difficult to follow. Therefore a few words need first to be said about the intellectual context within which Pope writes. In order to simplify matters a little I have chosen to focus discussion on the contrasting ideas of two extremely influential thinkers, Lord Shaftesbury and Thomas Hobbes, whose writings Pope knew. These philosophers put forward totally opposed views of Man, and it is true to say that in the early eighteenth century there was a fierce controversy between the 'Shaftesburian' and 'Hobbesian' ways of thinking. (Other figures such as Francis Hutcheson, a follower of Shaftesbury, and Bernard Mandeville, a disciple of Hobbes, continued the debate, and Jonathan Swift also engaged with it in Book Four of *Gulliver's Travels*, 1726). Against this

---

* Pope's 'Man', of course, is the species *Homo sapiens*, which includes both male and female, referred to throughout as 'he'. In order to avoid confusion I shall follow the same convention in this chapter.

background we may see that Pope's poem is not just turning traditional ideas into verse, but is debating the controversial issues of his day.

(i) The Intellectual Context

As twentieth-century readers we have lost touch with the things that once made *An Essay on Man* such an exciting work. We must remember that Pope was writing for a generation still reeling from the discoveries of Sir Isaac Newton, whose principle of 'gravity' made it clear that God had not merely created the universe, but was at all times sustaining it by a simple and beautiful law (the same law which held the planets in their orbits was the one that caused an apple to fall to the ground). It was a time when man's perceptions were expanding in thrilling new ways: developments in the telescope and microscope were revealing previously hidden worlds which could stimulate the writer's imagination. Joseph Addison, for instance, in his widely read *Spectator* essays on 'The Pleasures of the Imagination' (1712), compared the vast size of the galaxy with the tiny pores on a creature 'a hundred times less than a mite' and went on to discuss how these infinite distances of the universe stretched the human mind:

Nay, we might yet carry it farther, and discover in the smallest particle of this little world, a new inexhausted fund of matter, capable of being spun out into another universe.

(*Spectator* 420)

Such speculations, far from challenging religion, appeared to confirm the infinite power and wisdom of God, to the extent that a flourishing brand of theology (known as 'Physico-Theology') set out to make the 'Book of Nature' (i.e. the natural world) a kind of religious text through which Man might come to know and love his creator. Even so simple a thing as a duck's webbed feet could be evidence of how God in his infinite wisdom has perfectly adapted every creature for its life on earth.

The ancient notion of 'the Great Chain of Being' still flourished during the seventeenth and eighteenth centuries. According to this doctrine, the whole of creation was a single fabric made up of every living thing. The system was ordered in a strict hierarchy from the lowest forms of plant life to the highest angelic intelligences. A famous description of the chain (which Pope certainly knew) occurs in Milton's *Paradise Lost* (1667), where the angel Raphael tells Adam about the universe:

> O Adam, one almighty is, from whom
> All things proceed, and up to him return,
> If not depraved from good, created all
> Such to perfection, one first matter all,
> Indued with various forms, various degrees
> Of substance, and in things that live, of life;
> But more refined, more spirituous, and pure,
> As nearer to him placed
>
> (*Paradise Lost*, v, 469–76)

It was believed that the chain was completely unbroken and consisted of a vast number of infinitely small gradations. This is Addison again:

> The whole Chasm in Nature, from a Plant to a Man, is filled up with diverse Kinds of Creatures, rising one over another, by such a gentle and easie Ascent, that the little Transitions and Deviations from one Species to another, are almost insensible.
>
> (*Spectator* 519)

Addison goes on to quote the philosopher John Locke (the thinker who had perhaps the greatest influence on eighteenth-century English literature). Locke had given a similar account of the unity of the created world in his *Essay Concerning Human Understanding* (1689). The wonderful integration of all things was for him clear proof of 'the magnificent harmony of the universe, and the great design and infinite goodness of the architect'. Phrases like these were a common currency in the period. Those who believed the world to be a harmonious structure tended to argue that human values (Truth, Goodness, Beauty, Virtue etc.) were not mere subjective notions, but had an objective meaning within the 'rightness' of the system.

Perhaps the most influential English writer to develop the 'universal system' idea in the direction of morality and human behaviour was Lord Shaftesbury (1671–1713). In his *Characteristicks* (1711) he presents an idealizing and benevolent view of society. According to this, Man takes his place within God's best-possible 'S Y S T E M of all things' and naturally makes the good of others his own good. Nature gives him a sixth sense, called the 'moral sense', which expresses itself through a person's 'natural affections' (his instinctive love for his fellow-men). The Shaftesburian Man practises virtue for its own sake, and instead of relying on some outside force to regulate his actions, finds his own nature the best moral guide. Honesty and truth are beautiful, in that they express a person's harmony with 'universal Nature'.

77

Set against what we can call this 'idealist' viewpoint, there was another strain of thought which was set in total opposition to any concept of universal benevolence. Instead of establishing a harmonious universal system and then locating Man's place within it, this 'materialist' view took the internal nature of Man as its starting point. It saw the determining factor as matter, rather than divine spirit. This is the procedure adopted by Thomas Hobbes (1588–1679) in his controversial *Leviathan* (1651). Hobbes took the view that man as a species is by nature selfish and is impelled by his passions towards satisfying these drives and achieving his desires. Far from being 'parts of one stupendous whole' (*Essay on Man*, i, 267), humanity is a collection of individuals each pursuing what is 'good to himself' (good and evil, for Hobbes, merely mean 'good for me' or 'bad for me'). Self-preservation is the key to the behaviour of the human organism, and it is natural that a person will wish to dominate others. The implications of Hobbes's use of the term 'Nature' are completely opposed to Shaftesbury's. Where Shaftesbury believed that Man was by nature sociable and benevolent, Hobbes saw the natural state of Man as one of anarchy, a war of 'every man against every man'.

Although Hobbes had a considerable influence on literature (it can be seen, for instance, in the work of Milton and Swift), his materialist philosophy of 'self-love' was considered by many early eighteenth-century writers to be antagonistic to religion and the dignity of Man. (To many people those phrases meant much the same thing.) We can easily understand why people thought that Hobbes's views undermined moral and religious principles, since Hobbesian natural man owes nothing to anything outside himself (whether law, religion, or society, or something abstract such as Truth or Duty). According to Hobbes's view of society, men join together through fear, not love. Sociability and virtue are unnatural, and human institutions are set up only to prevent natural anarchy from taking over. Within such a society an individual is not bound to obey the law if it does not suit him, and he is only impelled to keep a promise when the other person has a sanction against him. It is up to the individual to choose whether he wishes to tell the truth or not.

We can see that the Hobbesian system makes logical sense, in that its principles are consistently followed through to their conclusions. And the same goes for the system of 'universal harmony'. There appears in fact to be no easy way of reconciling one viewpoint with the other, because they start from completely different assumptions. When Pope came to write *An Essay on Man* he felt he was entering 'a mighty maze!' (i, 6), and it is easy to see why.

In his brief introduction to the design of the poem he confesses to the reader:

If I could flatter myself that this Essay has any merit, it is in steering betwixt the extremes of doctrines seemingly opposite

We notice that he inserts the word *seemingly*. Clearly Pope thinks that doctrines which appear irreconcilable need not be, even though they represent *extremes*, and for him the species *Homo sapiens* is the common denominator. For Pope, Man is torn between matter and spirit, materialism and idealism, between a belief in the needs and drives of his own flesh and a conviction that he is more than just atoms in motion. This stress on the 'paradoxical' (i.e. contradictory) nature of Man is what most clearly separates Pope from both Shaftesbury and Hobbes. He is neither an idealist nor a materialist, but sees these 'doctrines seemingly opposite' as meeting in the paradox of Man. Inside each individual is being fought a continuous struggle to hold together the various aspects of his nature.

In no area is this more clear than in the question of knowledge: can we know only measurable, physical things? In raising this question, *An Essay on Man* becomes a poem about knowledge and its limits. In the prefatory 'Argument' to Epistle One, Pope admits that Man's place in creation has '*Ends* and *Relations* to him unknown', and at i, 18 he asks rhetorically: 'What can we reason, but from what we know?' Yet Book One celebrates those same '*Ends* and *Relations*' within the scheme of creation. There seems to be a contradiction here. How can a man (even a poet) located at a single point along the whole system grasp the beauty and purpose of the whole? How can Pope 'know' what God's design is?

The answer is, I think, that Pope has two kinds of 'knowledge' in mind: what we know from *experience* (what is called 'empirical' knowledge), and what our *reason* tells us must be the case, but which we cannot know from personal experience. Hobbes, not surprisingly, denied there could be anything except *empirical* knowledge, whereas Shaftesbury placed emphasis on Man's innate *rational* knowledge; truth for Hobbes was confined to what we experience, for Shaftesbury it was universal. Pope is aware of the claims of both kinds of knowledge and he exploits the tensions and contradictions between them. We know through our reason that we live in a universal system perfectly designed by God, but our empirical knowledge is confined to our own limited sphere. In other words, Man is capable of appreciating through his *reason* the whole system of creation (in this he is akin to the angels); but as far as *experience* goes he cannot deviate from his own tiny link in the chain (in this he is akin to the lower animals). For Pope, therefore, Man is a contradictory creature placed between spirit and matter:

> In doubt to deem himself a God, or Beast;
> In doubt his Mind or Body to prefer
>
> (ii, 8–9)

This dilemma, Pope implies, has faced Man ever since the Garden of Eden. At the opening of the *Essay* he sees himself as confronting a 'Garden, tempting with forbidden fruit' (i, 8, alluding to the Tree of Knowledge which brought Man's fall), and some of the poem's most memorable lines are those which set limits on our knowledge ('Know then thyself, presume not God to scan; / The proper study of Mankind is Man', ii, 1–2). In that first garden Eve was dissatisfied with her limited place in creation and wished to experience a 'higher' state. She thought that eating the fruit of knowledge would transform her into a godlike being, but how wrong she was. Her deadly adventure was the prime example of a man attempting to trespass beyond his allotted place in the Scale of Creation, and her combination of pride and foolishness lies behind the whole of Pope's *Essay on Man*. Each time he castigates our pride ('In Pride, in reas'ning Pride, our error lies', i, 123) or folly ('Fools!', 'Weak, foolish man!' etc.) he has in mind the figure of Eve, our first parent, and her proud, foolish adventure into forbidden knowledge.

(ii) The Poem

The underlying assumption behind Epistle I ('Of the Nature and State of Man, with respect to the UNIVERSE') is clearly stated in lines 43–8:

> Of Systems possible, if 'tis confest
> That Wisdom infinite must form the best,
> Where all must full or not coherent be,
> And all that rises, rise in due degree;
> Then, in the scale of reas'ning life, 'tis plain
> There must be, somewhere, such a rank as Man

The logical construction (*if . . ., Then . . . 'tis plain there must be . . .*) signals that this knowledge is not empirical, since it is being reached through reasoning rather than personal experience. The line of Pope's thought here is traditional: if we accept that God created the world, then because he is perfect and all-good his creation must likewise be the best possible. It must therefore be complete in every degree without any gaps (otherwise there would be areas of emptiness and the whole would not *cohere*), and also without any duplication (otherwise some parts would be superfluous). It follows that every point in the scale must touch, but not overlap with, the point above and below, to make a seamless whole. Man's place, therefore, is ordained somewhere within this scale, between the highest angels and the lowest forms of sentient life, and though the barrier closing him off on either side is infinitesimal, it is impossible to cross:

> See, thro' this air, this ocean, and this earth,
> All matter quick, and bursting into birth.
> Above, how high progressive life may go!
> Around, how wide! how deep extend below!
> Vast chain of being, which from God began,
> Natures aethereal, human, angel, man,
> Beast, bird, fish, insect! what no eye can see,
> No glass can reach! from Infinite to thee,
> From thee to Nothing! – On superior pow'rs
> Were we to press, inferior might on ours:
> Or in the full creation leave a void,
> Where, one step broken, the great scale's destroy'd:
> From Nature's chain whatever link you strike,
> Tenth or ten thousandth, breaks the chain alike.

(i, 233–46)

Within this vast system nothing can move out of its place. Every being is fitted with the abilities that ideally suit it, and so it is ridiculous for Man to envy the astonishing capacities of 'lower' creatures:

> Why has not Man a microscopic eye?
> For this plain reason, Man is not a Fly.
> Say what the use, were finer optics giv'n,
> T'inspect a mite, not comprehend the heav'n?
> Or touch, if tremblingly alive all o'er,
> To smart and agonize at ev'ry pore?
> Or quick effluvia darting thro' the brain,
> Die of a rose in aromatic pain?

(i, 193–200)

That brilliant final line, with its fusion of agony and ecstasy, the beautiful and the grotesque, captures in a single image the danger of Man wishing to exceed his capacities. He might consider himself limited, but in fact he is beautifully adapted for his life, and any expansion or heightening of his senses could bring torture and destruction.

Reading passages like these, we may feel that Pope is simply reducing and constricting Man's options. Some of his regular words of command (e.g. 'Submit!', 'Cease then!') appear to hold mankind back, fix him in his place rather than unfold exciting new possibilities. But it would be wrong to think of Pope's system as a static one. It may obey the 'gen'ral laws' of Nature (i, 146), but Nature here is a changing landscape in unpredictable weather. Life needs both 'show'rs and sunshine' (i, 152), and just as 'plagues or earthquakes' are natural occurrences, so in the moral world are evil and destructiveness ('a Borgia, or a Catiline', i, 156). The world inside Man is a stormy one, with the passions seen as equivalent to the contending elements in nature. Pope's 'Order', therefore, is not a suppression of the passions and energies but a harnessing of them, like the tension kept by the changing weather-patterns of the globe:

> Better for Us, perhaps, it might appear,
> Were there all harmony, all virtue here;
> That never air or ocean felt the wind;
> That never passion discompos'd the mind:
> But A L L subsists by elemental strife;
> And Passions are the elements of Life.
> The gen'ral O R D E R, since the whole began,
> Is kept in Nature, and is kept in Man.

(i, 165–72)

Of course, if the whole is a perfect system there is a danger that what is wrong or evil will be tolerated, or even sanctioned. Just as in the natural world an earthquake killing thousands of people might be seen as an Act of God, so morally we may be told we have to endure wrongs and injustices because they are a part of the Way Things Are. Pope admits as much:

> Respecting Man, whatever wrong we call,
> May, must be right, as relative to all.

(i, 51–2)

It is that easy and insidious shift from *may* to *must* which exposes the dangers of this line of thinking. Life's possibilities easily become necessities, doubts give way before certainties, questions are dispelled by answers. Pope brings the first epistle to its climax with a rousing assertion of the rightness of the world overriding all mankind's negatives by the all-embracing positive of the divine plan:

> All Nature is but Art, unknown to thee;
> All Chance, Direction, which thou canst not see;
> All Discord, Harmony, not understood;
> All partial Evil, universal Good:
> And, spite of Pride, in erring Reason's spite,
> One truth is clear, 'Whatever IS, is RIGHT.'

(i, 289–94)

It is almost as though there are two separate vocabularies: the language of Man (unknowing, unseeing, uncomprehending) and the Word of God (all-knowing, all-seeing, all-comprehending). Luckily for Pope's poetry, it is usually the former that he stresses.

As if to counteract the all-embracing certainties he has just announced, Pope begins the second epistle ('Man, with respect to Himself, as an Individual') with all the uncertainties of a creature precariously set on a narrow neck of land between two mighty oceans ('this isthmus of a middle state', i, 3), torn between the conflicting impulses of his nature. This is the contradictory world that Pope relishes:

> Chaos of Thought and Passion, all confus'd;
> Still by himself abus'd, or disabus'd;
> Created half to rise, and half to fall;
> Great lord of all things, yet a prey to all;
> Sole judge of Truth, in endless Error hurl'd:
> The glory, jest, and riddle of the world!

(ii, 13–18)

In these lines Pope sees human nature as chaotic, with Man's mental and emotional life (*Thought* and *Passion*) *all confus'd*. In the course of the second epistle Pope tries to disentangle this confusion and see the mechanism behind our actions. He does this by separating out two principles, *Self-love* and *Reason*:

> Two Principles in human nature reign;
> Self-love to urge, and Reason, to restrain;
> Nor this a good, nor that a bad we call,
> Each works its end, to move or govern all

(ii, 53–6)

These forces pull Man in opposite directions. It is almost as though Pope were thinking of them in physical terms, like the magnetic powers which science saw throughout the physical world. Just as the earth, like any magnet, has two opposing poles, and the smallest particles of

83

matter contain positive and negative charges, so Man himself operates by the interaction of contrasting principles.

Pope's terminology here may confuse us, since he is identifying the opposition between self-love and social love as being one between passion and reason. The passions, he says, are 'Modes of Self-love' (ii, 93), in other words they represent the impulse towards self-preservation and the fulfilling of a person's desires. In contrast, reason here means something like 'the ability to recognize a wider good than the self and to make assessments and choices in accord with it'. This may seem complicated, but the distinction is clear: our *passions* (hate, pride, desire, anger etc.) well up inside us and express our selfish urges; they can only be restrained or directed by *reason*, which keeps reminding us that there are other people in the world besides us, and other purposes in life beyond merely satisfying our passions. Once this contrast is appreciated, then Pope's argument is straightforward:

> Self-love, the spring of motion, acts the soul;
> Reason's comparing balance rules the whole.
> Man, but for that, no action could attend,
> And, but for this, were active to no end

(ii, 59–62)

It should be noted that throughout the passage ii, 53–92 'that' refers to *Self-love* and 'this' to *Reason* (the convention being that 'that' is the earlier of two things mentioned, while 'this' is the later). In line 76, therefore, reason is 'more watchful', and self-love is 'more strong'. Pope makes it clear, however, that either of these principles can be destructive if it has the field to itself. If Man lacks the driving-force of passion he will have no inner impulse and will simply be a rotten vegetable:

> Fix'd like a plant on his peculiar spot,
> To draw nutrition, propagate, and rot

(ii, 63–4)

But if passion possesses him to the exclusion of reasonable, sociable feelings, then this pure selfishness will destroy others along with himself:

> Or, meteor-like, flame lawless thro' the void,
> Destroying others, by himself destroy'd.

(ii, 65–6)

The secret is to recognize that human motives are often mixed, and that Man cannot entirely divorce his own good from the good of his species (global pollution, for example, is finally everybody's problem). Where the Roman stoic philosophers tended to denigrate the passions, aiming to achieve a kind of supreme indifference to them (*apatheia*), Pope challenges this as 'lazy Apathy' (ii, 101) and declares that 'strength of mind is Exercise, not Rest' (ii, 104). Passion is the driving-force of life, but we need the map ('card') of reason to give us a sense of direction:

> On life's vast ocean diversely we sail,
> Reason the card, but Passion is the gale
>
> (ii, 107–8)

The drives and instincts of the self are vital, and the passions (whether of pain or pleasure) give 'all the strength and colour of our life' (ii, 122).

In order to confirm the passions as the power-source of life, Pope goes on to develop his theory of the 'ruling Passion' (ii, 138). We each have, he says, one passion which tends to dominate our character. It is 'the Mind's disease' and grows along with us, but because it is part of our nature, reason can do little more than 'rectify' it (ii, 163). Fortunately every vice tends to have an equivalent virtue related to it, and this is where reason can turn the bias from evil to good (ii, 195–7). Ambition, for example, can be diverted towards patriotism (ii, 201–2).

For all the colours that Pope sees in life, he is keen to remind us that there remains the black and white of vice and virtue, however intermingled they might often be (ii, 207–14). But few of us are virtuous or vicious 'in th'extreme' (ii, 232) and Pope glances humorously at Man's tendency to familiarize himself with vice, seen as a gradual journey northwards. Vice is always further on, and we never think we have reached it (ii, 219–30). Pope will have nothing to do with Hobbes's idea that good and evil are merely subjective; they objectively exist as surely as the North and South poles exist on our planet, and Man can move towards one or the other. The 'North' may *appear* a relative term ('at York, 'tis on the Tweed;/In Scotland, at the Orcades . . .', ii, 222–3), but the pole is there exercising its magnetic influence on us and we need reason's 'card' to chart our position.

Epistle Three ('Man, with respect to Society') moves from the internal tensions within human nature to consider the principles operating when individuals join together to form societies. Once again Pope sees the selfish and sociable instincts as combining ('Nothing made wholly for *itself*, nor yet wholly for *another*', he says, summarizing the argument of lines 27–48). Once again the chain-image (here the 'chain of Love', iii, 7) allows him to assert the interconnectedness of things, viewing society as a 'sea of Matter' (iii, 19) formed from the combination of atomic particles:

> See plastic Nature working to this end,
> The single atoms each to other tend,
> Attract, attracted to, the next in place
> Form'd and impell'd its neighbour to embrace.
> See Matter next, with various life endu'd,
> Press to one centre still, the gen'ral Good.

(iii, 9–14)

God cannot therefore be expected to intervene in the personal fate of an individual. Man may selfishly believe that nature exists to delight and comfort *him*, but 'The fur that warms a monarch, warm'd a bear' (iii, 44). God's creation is interdependent, indeed it is a structure of 'mutual Wants', from which comes 'mutual Happiness' (iii, 112), and nothing can love itself alone: marriage, the family, the tribe, the nation, the race – at each point the 'int'rest' (iii, 146) is extended outwards from the self.

Pope's own footnote to line 147 describes the 'state of Nature' as being 'SOCIAL', and in saying this he consciously dismisses Hobbes's natural state of 'a war of every man against every man'. Pope in fact pictures the State of Nature as a Golden Age, with all things bonded together in a union of interest, where there could be no distinction between self-love and social ('Union the bond of all things, and of Man', iii, 150). Unlike Shaftesbury, however, Pope places this state of nature firmly in the past, and the dark picture he paints of 'the man of times to come' (iii, 161) suggests that he is thinking about the great gulf which opened up with the Fall of Man and Cain's murder of his brother Abel:

> [Man], foe to Nature, hears the gen'ral groan,
> Murders their species, and betrays his own.
> But just disease to luxury succeeds,
> And ev'ry death its own avenger breeds;
> The Fury-passions from that blood began,
> And turn'd on Man a fiercer savage, Man.

(iii, 163–8)

It is a rather Hobbesian picture of civil disorder, with Man warring against his own kind, and it highlights Pope's departure from Shaftesbury, who underplayed Man's fallen nature and his capacity for destructive violence. But Pope is not taking Hobbes's line either, since he sees these passions as a betrayal of (rather than a response to) our true natures. For Pope this is *not* the natural state of Man.

However, when he comes to describe how human societies are formed Pope follows Hobbes closely, seeing the key impulses as fear and self-preservation:

> So drives Self-love, thro' just and thro' unjust,
> To one Man's pow'r, ambition, lucre, lust:
> The same Self-love, in all, becomes the cause
> Of what restrains him, Government and Laws . . .
> How shall he keep, what, sleeping or awake,
> A weaker may surprise, a stronger take?
> His safety must his liberty restrain:
> All join to guard what each desires to gain.
> Forc'd into virtue thus by Self-defence,
> Ev'n Kings learn'd justice and benevolence
>
> (iii, 269–80)

But just as we feel Pope is taking the cynical Hobbesian view, he adds an extra couplet which turns his argument into a characteristic paradox:

> Self-love forsook the path it first pursu'd,
> And found the private in the public good.
>
> (iii, 281–2)

The original impetus may have been selfish, but the habit of social living has caused Man to identify his own good with that of his fellow-men. In other words, a process of education has taken place and Man has managed to recover something of that sociability of which he was originally capable. Both Hobbes and Shaftesbury imply that Man is *destined*, for good or ill, to act in accordance with the nature of the species (driven either by Hobbesian Self-love or Shaftesburian sociability). Pope recognizes both these impulses, but he resists the determinist implications. For him, living within society is an educational experience, forcing an individual to compromise and think of others. It teaches him to accept society's sanctions and values.

Both Hobbes and Shaftesbury, of course, recognized that human reason had a part to play. But here again Pope differs from both of them: Hobbes's 'reason' is an ability to make selfish calculations, Shaftesbury's 'reason' is an idealized principle of harmony and rightness within the universe. Pope's 'reason', however, is more hard-working and self-disciplining. It has to be worked at, is sometimes weak or treacherous, but it is the only thing we have to prevent us sinking to an animal level.

The fourth and final epistle ('Man, with respect to *Happiness*') considers humanity's endless quest for happiness in this life. Whether it takes the form of active pleasure or a more passive contentment, this is 'our being's end and aim' (iv, 1). It is also for Pope the great leveller in society. It cannot be dependent on rank or material possessions, since these differ widely from person to person, whereas 'Bliss is the same in subject or in king' (iv, 58) and cancels out all the inequalities in life. (Pope is returning to his earlier argument at ii, 261–70.) Its satisfactions must therefore lie in something equally attainable by a beggar and a king. That 'something' is virtue, which Pope sees as the acceptance of God's providential scheme:

> Who sees and follows that great scheme the best,
> Best knows the blessing, and will most be blest.

(iv, 95–6)

But what about evil? How is it that in this world vice often succeeds and virtue ends badly? Such accidents, cruelties and injustices should be seen, Pope argues, as deviations in nature, just as moral evil is a deviation of the human will (iv, 111–12). But it may be that what appears a 'deviation' turns out to be part of a wider good (like the Fall of Man, which served in the end to bring Christ's love and redemption of the human race). God therefore may allow change, deviation or loss, and it is not for us to conclude that the resulting 'ill' means that the providential system has broken down:

> We just as wisely might of Heav'n complain,
> That righteous Abel was destroy'd by Cain

(iv, 117–18)

Man is in a world where laws of nature operate and may be destructive (like the volcanic fires of Mount Etna, iv, 123–4). But it is ridiculous to think that God will miraculously intervene in individual cases:

> When the loose mountain trembles from on high,
> Shall gravitation cease, if you go by?

(iv, 127–8)

God does not directly *cause* ills, because He does not *make* things happen (otherwise God would merely be 'Fate'). He creates and guides a benign universal system, but He does not keep stopping it so that individuals will never suffer. Man should not judge the whole from the parts – particularly from the parts that affect him personally.

By the time Pope returns at line 145 to his famous statement from the end of Epistle I ('Whatever IS, is R I G H T'), we begin to see that this is not the emptily optimistic remark it at first appeared. Its terseness remains disconcerting, but we now recognize that Pope is not dismissing tragedies, accidents or evils. In themselves they *are* tragic and evil (and

88

Pope had plenty of experience of both) and it is right that a person should cry, pray or be angry. On this immediate human level Pope remains very much a realist. What he says is that it is wrong to move from personal grief and despair to the accusation of God, or to the conclusion that the world is meaningless.

As Pope moves to the end of his poem, therefore, he returns to his conviction that an individual is part of mankind, just as mankind in turn is part of something much greater. Gathering all his themes together, he returns to the 'chain of Love' image. The immense interlinked fabric leaves nothing isolated or private; at every point things touch and connect:

> that Chain which links th'immense design,
> Joins heav'n and earth, and mortal and divine;
> Sees, that no being any bliss can know,
> But touches some above, and some below

(iv, 333–6)

Far from dismissing the personal and human scale of things, Pope knows that it is within our small part of the chain that we have to work. In our own human relationships we act out in miniature those principles of mutual dependence and sympathy which keep the whole system going:

> Never elated, while one man's oppress'd;
> Never dejected, while another's bless'd

(iv, 323–4)

Pope ends the *Essay* with the passage we looked at in chapter two. The pebble of 'Self-love' is thrown into the lake, disturbing the level calm of the water. But from that moment its ripples spread outwards, to friend, parent, neighbour, country, and to the whole human race:

> Self-love thus push'd to social, to divine,
> Gives thee to make thy neighbour's blessing thine.
> Is this too little for the boundless heart?
> Extend it, let thy enemies have part:
> Grasp the whole worlds of Reason, Life, and Sense,
> In one close system of Benevolence:
> Happier as kinder, in whate'er degree,
> And height of Bliss but height of Charity.

(iv, 353–60)

But we should remember that this passage represents Pope's ideal, not his description of the way things are. We have to balance its optimistic tone against the poem's regular reminders of Man's folly and pride. Pope's supposed optimism in this poem lies in his hopes for Man, not in what he sees around him. He knows that his ideals will always be defeated by the contradictoriness of human nature, and so in the poem's final line we are reminded of the message which underpins the whole of the *Essay*:

And all our Knowledge is, OURSELVES TO KNOW.

9. *Epistle to Burlington*

By 1731 Pope had been a friend of Richard Boyle, Earl of Burlington, for some fifteen years, ever since the latter had been a young man newly returned from Italy, an enthusiastic admirer of the sixteenth-century architect Andrea Palladio and determined to establish 'Palladian' taste in England. Palladianism was a rediscovery of the ancient proportions of classical architecture, a style adapted not to rambling palaces, but to country houses and buildings of a more human scale. By 1731 Burlington was building a villa, Chiswick House (nowadays open to the public), strictly in the style of Palladio and designed (along with the gardens) by his friend William Kent, who lived at Chiswick until his death. Burlington himself was active as an architect and was responsible for, among other buildings, the Assembly Rooms at York. (According to some critics his exteriors were better than his interiors.) He engaged in public works, was a generous patron and friend to artists and musicians, and ran deeply into debt. When completed, Chiswick House with its gardens was to embody the tastes and principles of the Burlington circle, not just through the architecture and gardening but in terms of a certain kind of lifestyle centred on friendship, hospitality and good conversation, life lived according to a human scale where man would be measured not against grandeur or ceremony, but as he expressed an inner living principle which drew all aspects of his life into harmony. Though it appears on the surface to be a poem about architecture and gardening, the *Epistle to Burlington* is really an assertion of this deeper principle underlying civilized life itself.

What is this principle? As the poem begins, it would appear to be 'Taste'. The half-title of the first edition is *Of Taste*, and the term appears four times in the first two paragraphs. When we examine the nuances of its use we see that Pope is playing satirically with various contexts for the word. First is the spendthrift, who has so much money that he wastes it on what 'he ne'er can taste' (4). Here the word *taste* obviously means 'to savour or appreciate': this prodigal collects widely and variously, but not according to his own principles. He allows others to choose for him so that nothing in his collection ends up being really *his*, no more than his wife or whore. The next figure, Virro, has painted, built and planted 'Only to show how many Tastes he wanted' (14). Here the word is placed

91

in the plural, suggesting that it is not a principle, just a succession of attempts gone wrong. The third use of the term is the voice of the 'Daemon' who whispers into Sir Visto's ear: 'Visto! have a Taste' (16). We note that here for the second time it rhymes with 'waste', but now it has undertones of the serpent's temptation of Eve in the Garden of Eden when he urged her to taste the forbidden fruit. Visto is obviously heading for ruin. Yet again, *Taste* does not come from within, but strikes as a kind of whim in which the man's wealth allows him to indulge. The final use of the word (line 17) is similar, but now it is not the devil but Heaven which 'visits with a Taste the wealthy fool'. None of these four phrases has presented taste as a *principle*. We have seen it pluralized, turned into a verb, and twice as *a Taste*. What Pope does at the beginning of his poem, therefore, is to set up various false notions of taste, so that he can then assert what true taste is.

But just as we might expect him to do this, Pope holds his fire. He turns to address Burlington directly (line 23) in terms of his architectural interests and the 'rules' (25) set out in his grand publications *The Designs of Inigo Jones* (1727) and *The Buildings of Andrea Palladio* (1730). His friend is not to be blamed because his 'noble rules / Fill half the land with Imitating Fools' (25–6). Obviously taste is not simply a matter of following rules, no matter how noble or authoritative. The point is well-made and humorously illustrated, but still Pope holds back, now pushing the argument a little deeper to a principle which underlies that of taste:

> Something there is more needful than Expence,
> And something previous ev'n to Taste – 'tis Sense:
> Good Sense, which only is the gift of Heav'n
>
> (41–3)

In rejecting mere rules and taking his stand on the principle of *Good Sense*, Pope is attempting to establish a firm foundation. In his great *Dictionary* (1755) Dr Johnson quoted this very passage to illustrate the word *sense* as meaning 'understanding; soundness of faculties; strength of natural reason'. In other words, the term relates not just to the way we perceive things through the senses, but to how we form ideas from them and what decisions we make on the basis of them. *Good Sense* is not, in other words, a faculty in itself, but a healthy state of *all* the faculties, which allows strong and clear communication from perception, to understanding, to action. Hence it is regularly associated with light and is sometimes called 'natural light'. What sense is being distinguished from here is whimsy or fancifulness such as we met in the sylphs with their superficial and discoloured lights. The light of sense, says Pope, is different:

> Good Sense, which only is the gift of Heav'n,
> And tho' no science, fairly worth the sev'n:
> A Light, which in yourself you must perceive;
> Jones and Le Nôtre have it not to give.

(43–6)

In defining taste in terms of this notion of *Good Sense*, Pope is attempting to move it out of the area of whimsy or a purely personal fancy, and also to distinguish it from a slavish acceptance of some external authority, whether Inigo Jones in architecture or the great Versailles gardener Le Nôtre. It has to be personal, to the extent that it is an inner light, but it should be objectively valid too; after all, it is *the gift of Heav'n* and to that extent should be shared and appreciated by others. It draws together, therefore, the subjective and the objective, the personal and the general.

Now that Pope has got to this point in his argument it seems inevitable that he should confront once again the topic of 'Nature'. When we encountered it earlier in *An Essay on Criticism* (68–79) it was in terms of a literary work. Now the idea powerfully reappears as present in a garden landscape, but it is the same broad concept. Here 'Nature' is that tendency within each living thing to achieve its own inner form (the tendency of an oak to reach a shape different from that of a yew or beech, the tendency of a stream to find a path for itself through undulating ground). But the maker of a garden, says Pope, does not merely allow the process to go ahead randomly and confusedly; he intervenes to guide and develop this tendency. In planting a grove of trees, or in damming a stream to create a lake, this involves a degree of artifice (*Art*), but in this exercise the practical and the artistic meet. A huge bleak rectangle of water or a procession of trees in a straight line will deny nature, and the result will be monotonous, characterless and lifeless. A form too obviously imposed on nature will drain the life from it.

As in the natural world, so in human life and art, there must be some balance between spontaneous tendencies within and order and direction imposed from without. This principle is crucial to any understanding of Pope's poetry, and nowhere does it find more fervent expression than in the following passage, which seems to be merely about gardening, but which has application to any artistic creativity and to human life in general:

93

> Consult the Genius of the Place in all;
> That tells the Waters or to rise, or fall,
> Or helps th'ambitious Hill the heav'n to scale,
> Or scoops in circling theatres the Vale,
> Calls in the Country, catches opening glades,
> Joins willing woods, and varies shades from shades,
> Now breaks or now directs, th'intending Lines;
> Paints as you plant, and, as you work, designs.
>   Still follow Sense, of ev'ry Art the Soul,
> Parts answ'ring parts shall slide into a whole,
> Spontaneous beauties all around advance,
> Start ev'n from Difficulty, strike from Chance;
> Nature shall join you, Time shall make it grow
> A Work to wonder at – perhaps a STOW.
>
>   (57–70)

This passage deserves to be quoted at length because its power as a statement is in the way it develops momentum from line to line, communicating a sense of increasing enthusiasm as all these actions begin to show results. Note how the first four lines establish the basic iambic pentameter unit: as the subject rises and falls it is held and ordered. In the next two lines the poise is preserved, but here the lines pivot about a central pause (the *caesura*): '*Calls in* the Country,/*catches* opening glades,/ *Joins* willing woods,/and *varies* shades from shades'. The speed is increasing, the verbs and nouns balancing each other. In the following line these regularities are broken by a shift in the placing of the verbs: 'Now *breaks*/or now *directs*/th'intending Lines', a line which enacts the effect it describes by adjusting the rhythm and preventing monotony from creeping in. The following line similarly captures what Pope is saying about the way human activity and the activity of nature can work together: 'Paints *as you plant*, and, *as you work*, designs'. If we look at this line more closely, we can see that the human activity (*plant*, *work*) is framed by the activity of nature (*Paints*, *designs*) and the whole line takes on a satisfying arch-like shape (chiasmus) of A–B–C–B–A. Pope is conscious as he writes of how parts answer parts and everything slides into a whole. Here nature proves an enthusiastic partner, and the key perhaps lies in the driving-force throughout the passage of the many active verbs (*scoops*, *calls*, *catches*, *joins*, *varies*, *breaks*, *directs*, *paints*, *designs*). It is a living landscape which is taking shape, and presiding over the whole is the goddess Nature herself, a modest but co-operative figure who is all the more attractive for being scantily and intriguingly dressed:

> But treat the Goddess like a modest fair,
> Nor over-dress, nor leave her wholly bare;
> Let not each beauty ev'ry where be spy'd,
> Where half the skill is decently to hide.

(51–4)

This is the presiding spirit that haunts the glades, ponds and groves of Pope's ideal garden, and it is against this vision of a living, fertile, harmonious yet varied landscape that Pope goes on to measure the disasters of that false taste which ignores both sense and nature.

The figure who embodies this anti-nature is Timon, the wealthy owner of a grandiose mansion and spacious gardens upon which no amount of money has been spared. Timon's pride makes him believe that by creating a setting for himself of such size and magnificence he will appear to be great himself. The irony, Pope points out, is that the grander his surroundings the more belittled and ridiculous Timon will seem:

> his building is a Town,
> His pond an Ocean, his parterre a Down:
> Who but must laugh, the Master when he sees,
> A puny insect, shiv'ring at a breeze!
> Lo, what huge heaps of littleness around!

(105–9)

Timon, in striving for grandeur, has lost the human scale. In Pope's mind, as in his friend Swift's, pride is always associated with littleness because it so belittles man. In *Gulliver's Travels* Swift had shown the tiny Gulliver among the giant Brobdingnagians as being an insufferably vain little creature. No wonder, then, that Timon's villa 'brings all Brobdignag before your thought' (104). Hence Pope's unflattering reference to 'proud Versailles!' (71), the huge palace of the French kings. It is interesting to note that when the young poet Thomas Gray visited Versailles in 1739 he wrote to a friend: 'Well! and is this the great front of Versailles? What a huge heap of littleness!' Clearly he knew his Pope.

But at Timon's villa it is not just the scale that is wrong. The whole effect is monotonous:

> No pleasing Intricacies intervene,
> No artful wildness to perplex the scene;
> Grove nods at grove, each Alley has a brother,
> And half the platform just reflects the other.

(115–18)

95

Critical Studies: Poetry of Alexander Pope

Artful wildness is a rather perplexing idea, but this is exactly Pope's point, and we saw in the 'Genius of the Place' passage how art and nature can work together. But here the effect of the formal lines of trees nodding politely at each other is gently comic. As we move on, the passage becomes increasingly unsettling as Pope presents the *inverted Nature* of Timon's garden. Everything is odd and incongruous because its own nature has been either ignored or contradicted. The result is a brilliant exercise in the grotesque:

> The suff'ring eye inverted Nature sees,
> Trees cut to Statues, Statues thick as trees,
> With here a Fountain, never to be play'd,
> And there a Summer-house, that knows no shade;
> Here Amphitrite sails thro' myrtle bow'rs;
> There Gladiators fight, or die, in flow'rs;
> Un-water'd see the drooping sea-horse mourn,
> And swallows roost in Nilus' dusty Urn.

(119–26)

The nature of everything has been perverted, but Pope's art exercises its own weird creativity as he sets the scene before us. To imagine gladiators dying among flowers reveals a strange beauty underneath the comic. Once again Pope's creativity exploits the fantastic qualities in those he satirizes. The key here, of course, is *suffering*: it is finally an arid and uncomfortable landscape, with undertones of pain in the cruel pruning of the topiary trees, the suffocating summer-house and unwatered sea-horse, and the figure of the River Nile whose urn has dried up.

We note that there is no current of water here: everything is parched and infertile. In *Windsor Forest* Pope had used water to provide a kind of moving and connecting principle through that poem. Eighteenth-century gardens too could use water in this way, as in the magical landscape of Stourhead, Wiltshire. The garden (now owned by the National Trust) was begun in the 1740s by a significant figure for Burlington's circle, his banker Henry Hoare, and it was designed around underground springs which help to supply the lake. By an act of creative co-operation between art and nature, Hoare constructed a grotto around one of these, within which he placed the figure of a River God holding an urn, so designed that the spring runs out through the urn itself. Such an idea is not mere ingenuity: it declares the living principle within his landscape, and within the landscape of his mind and spirit. Hoare's letters during the creation of Stourhead often quote the *Epistle to Burlington*, and to understand the poem a visit to Stourhead is worth the whole of this chapter.

Timon's garden is an uncomfortable and unsettling place, and calling to visit him is an exhausting experience. Inside the house incongruity is again the keynote, and this theme is introduced by Pope in terms of 'Decorum', another term encountered in *An Essay on Criticism*. Here the outraging of decorum is exemplified by Timon's chapel and dining-room. In line 29 one of the blunders of false taste was to 'load some vain Church with old Theatric state', and this is exactly the nature of the chapel, a setting for 'all the Pride of Pray'r' (142), the alliteration pointing up the indecorum. The 'light quirks of Musick, broken and uneven' (143) show the disjointedness of a setting which is unsuited to its purposes, where again nothing properly fits. Once more Pope revels in this opportunity to press odd and discomforting suggestions from the words he uses:

> On painted Cielings you devoutly stare,
> Where sprawl the Saints of Verrio or Laguerre,
> On gilded clouds in fair expansion lie,
> And bring all Paradise before your eye.
> To rest, the Cushion and soft Dean invite,
> Who never mentions Hell to ears polite.

> (145–50)

In Timon's chapel, Heaven (French *ciel*) is just a painted *Cieling*, and in this place of devotion the phrase *devoutly stare* conveys a kind of blankness, a mere gaze which is met by the *sprawl* of the saints (one of a number of words in the poem conveying awkward or grotesque movement). The next line is calculatedly vague, with *gilded* merely echoing *painted*, and the phrase *fair expansion* made uneasy by the way it somehow becomes a euphemism for *sprawl*. The glib predictability of line 148 reminds us that it is only the eye which is involved here; and the final couplet immediately offers physical comfort and distraction. 'To rest, the Cushion', it says, almost in relief, before the Dean politely appears, the epithet *soft* surreptitiously transferred from the cushion to himself. The subtlety of suggestion in these lines is masterly.

If the chapel has the character of a theatre, then Timon's pompous dining-room resembles nothing so much as a pagan temple. Here the guest feels he is being offered up as some kind of sacrifice to the god of Timon's self-esteem, and it is this image through which Pope presents the meal:

97

> Is this a dinner? this a Genial room?
> No, 'tis a Temple, and a Hecatomb.
> A solemn Sacrifice, perform'd in state,
> You drink by measure, and to minutes eat.

(155–8)

A 'Hecatomb' was a pagan sacrifice involving the slaughter of a hundred oxen, and the rhythm of the lines captures the empty ritual of what ought to be a sociable and human occasion. Here the formal regularity echoes that of the garden outside, and the buffet is ornamented with figures that would better suit a water-garden:

> The rich Buffet well-colour'd Serpents grace,
> And gaping Tritons spew to wash your face.

(153–4)

The uncomfortable incongruity of these lines is literally 'grotesque' (a term originally applied to paintings in grottoes and caves) as Pope's own footnote points out when it refers to 'the incongruity of *Ornaments* . where an open mouth ejects the water into a fountain, or where the shocking images of serpents, etc. are introduced in Grottos or Buffets'. This is the key to Pope's comic tactics in these scenes. The grotesque decor of the grotto has invaded the dining-tables, and the effect is weird and ridiculous.

At the climax of Pope's grumbling and cursing as he takes his leave of Timon, he distances himself from the scene in order to contemplate the paradox behind all his host's extravagances. The wider fact is that this spendthrift helps to provide employment for his labourers and servants. In some way even this massively tasteless enterprise serves a providential end. Pope draws further back still, almost with a sense of relief, to contemplate the dawn of a future age which he pictures in terms of fertility and fruition:

> Another age shall see the golden Ear
> Imbrown the Slope, and nod on the Parterre,
> Deep Harvests bury all his pride has plann'd,
> And laughing Ceres re-assume the land.

(173–6)

The unnatural aridity of Timon's physical and spiritual landscape will be replaced by a Golden Age (of golden cornfields) as nature returns in the form of the Roman goddess of the harvest. Timon's magnificence has been a usurpation.

Sounding just for a moment as though he wishes to erase human structures altogether, Pope is careful to end his poem, as he had done *Windsor Forest*, on a note of optimism and progress. Once more forests grow into navies (line 188), and in these final disappointing paragraphs the tone becomes declamatory and pompous. Pope is trying to distinguish a proper kind of *public* magnificence from the self-aggrandizing magnificence of Timon. However, the lines make the sort of grand gestures we have learned to be suspicious of, and Lord Burlington's rather modest interest in public architecture (he became a Commissioner for the building of Westminster Bridge in 1737) is transformed into a godlike power to command the elements:

> Bid Harbors open, public Ways extend,
> Bid Temples, worthier of the God, ascend;
> Bid the broad Arch the dang'rous Flood contain,
> The Mole projected break the roaring Main;
> Back to his bounds their subject Sea command,
> And roll obedient Rivers thro' the Land

(197–202)

In ending with this 'happy Britain' (203) theme, Pope has lost touch with those human needs and sensitivities which are so intricately explored in the rest of the poem. Timon had forgotten them, and now Pope is brushing them aside in order to evoke a kind of activity that has no place for the human figure. The individual human is given no room among these temples, broad acres and expensive projects, and Pope's urging of Burlington here has undertones of that earlier temptation to wrongful pride ('You too proceed!/. . . be whate'er Vitruvius was before:/Till Kings call forth th'Idea's of your mind', 191–5). We have only to compare the phrasing and rhythm of this passage with the 'Genius of the Place' episode (47–70) to sense that something is different; something is missing.

Up to line 176 the *Epistle to Burlington* is one of the finest examples both of Pope's flexible handling of verse and his insight into human nature. The final sections of the poem (177–204) are competent and serviceable, but lack the spider's-web sensitivity that his writing has at its finest. The reason probably is that Pope is here delivering his own message clearly and unequivocally, so that he is cut off from that area of paradoxical response which nourishes his verse. Pope writes at his best when he is charting the currents of human feeling in response to settings, incidents and objects that disconcert him. Violations of decorum,

99

misdirected energies, failures of perspective, impotent fantasies of power –these are the themes which inspire his subtlest writing. *Epistle to a Lady. Of the Characters of Women* allows him full scope to tackle the more complex and unsettling aspects of human behaviour.

10. *Epistle to a Lady*

Running through *Epistle to a Lady: Of the Characters of Women* is a single metaphor: that of painting. In his twenties Pope had taken up painting under the guidance of his friend Charles Jervas, one of the foremost portraitists of his day, and while living in Jervas's house in London he had worked at copying the canvases of both Jervas and Sir Godfrey Kneller (one of which survives: see Maynard Mack's *Alexander Pope, A life*, p. 91). In a letter Pope describes the opportunities this gave him for indulging himself in the intimate details of a woman's beauty:

Every Corner of an Eye, or Turn of a Nose or Ear, the smallest degree of Light or Shade on a Cheek, or in a dimple, have charms to distract me. I no longer look on Lord *Plausible* as ridiculous, for admiring a Lady's fine Tip of an Ear and pretty Elbow.

(Pope to Gay, 23 August 1713)

He is conscious that in trying to capture minute features he is being made to forget the more general and fundamental elements of an artwork: composition, disposition of the figure, firmness of line. Instead, such formal aspects have given way to a delight in tiny details and subtle shadings – the parts rather than the whole. The aesthetic (and as always for Pope, moral) issue raised here is: where does the 'truth' lie? In the effect of the whole? or in the lifelike parts? Should the artist strive to transcend distracting details in order to achieve a more generally powerful effect? Or attempt at all costs to catch transient but characteristic minutiae? This artistic debate, often centring on the role of colour in painting, had been a recurrent one in art criticism, and was to be most memorably expressed by Sir Joshua Reynolds in the fourth of his *Discourses on Art* (1771). In placing his *Epistle* within this debate, Pope is asking questions about how we assess the 'character' of somebody, and what goes to form such a 'character'. This takes him into a more profound area: how far is human nature predictable and consistent? Is there a continuum of something we may call a 'selfhood'? Are some people tragically doomed to repeat the same mistakes and pursue the same fantasies? What is the relationship between our sense of ourselves (and others) as fully composed wholes, and the quirks, oddities and obsessions which may be our individualizing characteristics? These are just some of

101

the questions that *Epistle to a Lady* raises, about art, literature and human nature.

The poem begins with what seems a rather offensive statement: 'Most Women have no Characters at all' (line 2). This is recalled as a remark of Martha Blount (the 'lady' to whom the poem is addressed), and nowadays it seems a crude and dismissive generalization. But in Pope's day the term 'character' was used to imply consistency, features which fitted suitably together and made sense in terms of the person's 'nature'. Having *no character* points to the unpredictableness and inconsistency of the women he is about to consider. After all, none of them is short on what we would today term 'character', but this is not what Pope is saying. Underneath it all, of course, lies the ancient idea that 'woman is fickle' (a traditional notion going back to Virgil and beyond). Pope enjoys playing with this idea, but what makes his portraits so fascinating is the way he locates this changeableness in deeper, more troubling aspects of the psyche, and relates it to wider themes about art and morality.

In order to highlight the uncertainties and ambivalences of his subject, Pope introduces in line 6 a deliberately wayward notion of *truth*:

> How many pictures of one Nymph we view,
> All how unlike each other, all how true!
> Arcadia's Countess, here, in ermin'd pride,
> Is there, Pastora by a fountain side:
> Here Fannia, leering on her own good man,
> Is there, a naked Leda with a Swan,

> (5–10)

'All how true!' is the kind of empty remark we might overhear in an art gallery. Which *is* the 'true' woman? – the person proudly swathed in furs, or the imitation shepherdess reclining by a fountain? The passage suggests that both are artificial posturings. Fannia raises more disturbing implications: she is first seen as the faithful wife (*leering* suggests the strain that this involves), but at the next moment is acting out a mythological rape as the nymph Leda, violated by Zeus who had assumed the form of a swan. (It had long been one of the most erotic subjects in art.) Which role is truer to the 'real' Fannia, domestic reality or a fantasy-life among the gods? Or does it perhaps tell us more about the ambiguous feelings of her husband, who may wish her publicly on show as the sweetly admiring consort, but privately painted as a victim of godlike sexual energy?

Having established this context of gesture, posture, role-playing, and a general sense of the elusiveness of 'truth', Pope the artist recognizes a challenge and can no longer hold himself back:

> Come then, the colours and the ground prepare!
> Dip in the Rainbow, trick her off in Air,
> Chuse a firm Cloud, before it fall, and in it
> Catch, ere she change, the Cynthia of this minute.

> (17–20)

The imagery of rainbow-beams and shifting clouds suggests that Pope is consciously adopting an impressionistic, sketch-book kind of art where the accumulation of telling detail will be more successful than a fully composed portrait.

The opening 156 lines of the *Epistle* bear this out by adapting their technique to catch the moods, inconsistencies and whims of these women. We hardly glimpse Rufa ('whose eye quick-glancing o'er the Park', 21) before she is gone (a victim of her own roving eye) and we settle for a moment on Sappho (Lady Mary Wortley Montagu) glimpsed at her toilette and at a masquerade, scenes so rapidly juxtaposed that the 'greazy task' of the one and the fragrance of the other begin to merge like dabs of watercolour to produce an unsettling mixture. With Silia the technique is to settle the tone (lines 29–32) and then shatter it with an exclamation ('Sudden, she storms! she raves!') like Belinda's sudden fury in *The Rape of the Lock*. Then the line is completed by another gesture, this time silent, monosyllabic and merciless ('You tip the wink'), which returns us to the language of eyes, as everything focuses mesmerically on the one spot:

> All eyes may see from what the change arose,
> All eyes may see – a Pimple on her nose.

> (35–6)

Our glance now falls on Papillia ('Butterfly') who 'wedded to her doating spark,/Sighs for the shades' (37–8). Her relationship with this showy, fashionable man and her longing for solitude are expressed in terms of sparkling light and relieving shade. But Papillia is unsettled wherever she is, and the park offers no relief: 'Oh odious, odious Trees!'(40).

These are the 'variegated Tulips' (41) of women, changeable and charming at the same time, and Pope's artistry attempts to capture the colourful details. But as if to introduce a contrasting mood or shade into his own picture, he turns to Calypso (45–52) who is not visualized in any way, but is disturbing and elusive none the less. She is also removed into the past tense, as though this ambiguous woman (odd, bewitching, mimicking, strange) could, without either beauty or virtue, arouse a mixture of alarm, awe and hate. It is not that in this picture positives clash with negatives, but that the negatives themselves do not fit together. Alarm, awe and hate are an uneasy combination. Pope conceals her from us like a hidden private memory, and it is appropriate perhaps that someone whose name means 'she who conceals' (Greek *kalypso*) should not be revealed to us through imagery.

After this 'shady' interlude, Narcissa (53–68) is introduced with a disturbing rhyme ('tolerably mild' – 'stew a child'), ideas which could hardly create a greater contrast of mood; and indeed Narcissa is caught between extremes of carnal pleasure and cold conscience. Pope gives us momentary glimpses of her in contrasting postures:

> Now deep in Taylor and the Book of Martyrs,
> Now drinking citron with his Grace and Chartres.
> Now Conscience chills her, and now Passion burns;
> And Atheism and Religion take their turns;
> A very Heathen in the carnal part,
> Yet still a sad, good Christian at her heart.

(63–8)

The brushstrokes once again merge into each other: *drinking citron* and being *deep in Taylor* become the same act of self-indulgence, and *his Grace* applies as much to an Archbishop as to the Duke of Wharton. Narcissa is unsettled and unsatisfied, a victim of Pope's antitheses, but even more of her own antithetical nature.

This theme is continued in Philomede (69–86), both peeress and 'punk' (prostitute), split between her head ('that noble Seat of Thought') and her 'Blood and Body', between her 'bosom' and her 'brain'. Pope is switching rapidly from one part of the figure to another, from one context to another, one role to another:

> Chaste to her Husband, frank to all beside,
> A teeming Mistress, but a barren Bride.

(71–2)

As these images flicker before us we begin to understand the moral message carried by Pope's technique. Philomede here, in playing so many roles, has confused them and got her priorities distorted. To be

104

frank (= 'open', with all that suggests) to everyone except her husband, to be chaste only to him, is to be neither chaste nor frank.

One theme running through these sketches is how easily a positive quality can become negative if it is misdirected or exaggerated. If Philomede exemplifies the former, then Flavia (87–100) illustrates the latter. Flavia's mind has been taken over by the formulae of romantic passion, and so her picture is created by a patchwork of phrases and stage-props from tragic romance:

> Nor asks of God, but of her Stars to give
> The mighty blessing, 'While we live, to live.'
> Then all for Death, that Opiate of the soul!
> Lucretia's dagger, Rosamonda's bowl.

(89–92)

But just as we begin to respond to these gestures of pathos, Pope cuts across our sympathies:

> Say, what can cause such impotence of mind?
> A Spark too fickle, or a Spouse too kind.

(93–4)

What may come over as powerful in drama or fiction turns out in reality to be mere *impotence* of mind. Once again intense emotions and positive qualities end up losing their power; they turn round destructively on their subject, just as Pope's lines turn round on themselves:

> With too much Spirit to be e'er at ease,
> With too much Quickness ever to be taught,
> With too much Thinking to have common Thought

(96–8)

The repeated pattern conveys the obsessiveness of Flavia's mind, the climax and anti-climax (pathos and bathos) of each line rises and falls until these ups and downs become predictable. The highly-sensitized Flavia ends by being her own victim, gaining pain from joy and winning death out of life. An idea that Keats's palate would savour becomes for Pope merely self-defeating:

> Who purchase Pain with all that Joy can give,
> And die of nothing but a Rage to live.

(99–100)

Purchase Pain and *die of nothing* are fine examples of Pope's ability to compress ironies into the briefest of phrases.

If the misdirection of energies is one of Pope's major themes, then his

105

own style in the poem consciously runs the risk of failing in the same way. It flirts with the haphazardness, the missing of targets, the possibilities for ironic reversal. By adopting a kind of mimickry, he allows himself to come unsettlingly close at times to making the style of these women his own. Atossa, for example, '*is*, whate'er she hates and ridicules' (120) and there is a danger that Pope will be the same:

> No Thought advances, but her Eddy Brain
> Whisks it about, and down it goes again . . .
> So much the Fury still outran the Wit,
> The Pleasure miss'd her, and the Scandal hit.

(121–8)

Such a missing of targets, a lack of steadiness, a dependence on chance, is exactly what Pope risks, and in returning to discuss his own style at this point he echoes those same lines about Atossa:

> Pictures like these, dear Madam, to design,
> Asks no firm hand, and no unerring line;
> Some wand'ring touch, or some reflected light,
> Some flying stroke alone can hit 'em right

(151–4)

It is as though in aiming at a moving target Pope is playing for high stakes and wants to draw attention to the adaptability of his style and his ability to score the odd bull's-eye. This is seen in the merciless way he picks off the chilling small-talk of Cloe, that prudent but heartless woman, the type (male or female) of all those who don't want to get involved:

> She, while her Lover pants upon her breast,
> Can mark the figures on an Indian chest;
> And when she sees her Friend in deep despair,
> Observes how much a Chintz exceeds Mohair.

(167–70)

Again the image is one of shifting eyes, the vision catching at surfaces, and this is exactly what Pope risks himself. After all, *pants upon her breast* is a hackneyed phrase, but in using it he is aware of its superficiality and is trying to convey something of the routineness in the sentimental situation that leaves Cloe bored. Nor does Pope attempt to penetrate beneath the surface of the *deep despair* of Cloe's friend. But the one brilliant stroke here is the way *sees* (line 169) moves in the next line to *observes*, and we realize that Cloe has seen *and* understood the situation.

If she had not understood, she would not have flinched away into small-talk (*observes* here means 'comments' and is not the result of genuine seeing, whereas *sees* in line 169 means both 'sees' *and* 'understands'). What I am trying to suggest is that Pope is risking sympathy with these women. He does not condone their excesses, but his imagination is able to identify with the emotion felt even by Cloe (who is one of the least 'sympathetic' figures). In giving us for a moment a sense of the stereotype lover (whose gestures she is probably bored with) and in revealing that Cloe can see and understand her friend, Pope is suggesting that she is superficial rather than shallow (and the difference is important). She lives a life on the surface because she cannot bear to confront the depths within her. With his *wand'ring touch* and *reflected light* Pope is writing some of his profoundest poetry – yet how easy it is to think he is being superficial himself.

We have seen how Pope's satirical technique in this poem, like the painterly technique he discusses, achieves its power through an ability to catch the small detail or momentary gesture, rather than attempt to compose a formal portrait. The one 'certain Portrait' is that of the Queen (181–90) whose vices have all been varnished over ('the same for ever!'), but we soon realize that this art is lifeless and empty, and we do not see *her* at all, just a swelling 'Robe of Quality' which hides everything from view. There is no detail, no movement, no life. In momentarily changing his technique Pope has made an effective satirical point.

One theme running through *Epistle to a Lady* has been a tragic one. The women who appear before us (people with considerable energy, wit, imagination and spirit) have each failed to direct these qualities to a positive end, and instead have become frustrated and self-defeating. Pope does not wish them to deny and repress their passionate natures (and he gives us Cloe as a warning against such repression), but to find some means of stabilizing and directing these qualities, so that they will become genuinely effective.

The word 'end' can mean both 'purpose' and 'ending'. The women in the poem 'end' badly or sadly partly because they have not directed their volatile natures to some worthwhile 'end'. Atossa, for example, is 'by the Means defeated of the Ends' (143), and the later pageant of veterans (235–48) have been 'fair to no purpose, artful to no end' (245). We should not be surprised, therefore, to see Pope towards the end of his poem sum up the purposelessness by showing how such figures end up. What is surprising is that his imagination creates out of this a strange witches' sabbath:

> As Hags hold Sabbaths, less for joy than spight,
> So these their merry, miserable Night;
> Still round and round the Ghosts of Beauty glide,
> And haunt the places where their Honour dy'd.

(239–42)

Restless to the last, the typical movement of the poem is brought to a swirling climax. These *Ghosts of Beauty* unsettlingly recall the sylphs of *The Rape of the Lock* with their concern for 'honour' and their disembodied beauty. But now they circle pointlessly. Even in old age these women are restless, enacting past rituals now drained of the magic they once had.

At this point Pope introduces the idea of fatigue in order to give a final negative turn to the dazzle and activity he has surveyed. Turning to Martha Blount (line 249) he welcomes her into the picture with a sense of relief, as the mild and sober light of the moon after the glare of the sun which, like the beauties of the day, 'flaunts and goes down, an unregarded thing' (252). She is 'blest with Temper' (257), that quality which tempers and regulates extremes; but not in a negative sense. It is placed in a context of constancy-through-time ('whose unclouded ray/Can make to morrow chearful as to day', 257–8) and is active in family relationships (sister, daughter, husband). It is true self-possession in all senses of the term, and is a genuine source of power. As the ideal type of 'Contradiction', Martha Blount achieves a blend of qualities (just like Pope's couplets, now working to convey balance). This is not some nondescript 'middle way' which is uncommitted and emptied of passion. Quite the contrary, it is an active and strenuous fusion of elements:

> Reserve with Frankness, Art with Truth ally'd,
> Courage with Softness, Modesty with Pride,
> Fix'd Principles, with Fancy ever new

(277–9)

This is above all a fusion of the constant and the shifting. The changeable women sketched in the *Epistle* lacked a constant heart, a selfhood which remained committed to principle beneath all the cravings, posturings and fantasies. With a proper sense of coming home, Pope identifies his own poetic procedure with the new dispensation of Martha Blount. *Art with Truth ally'd* declares the distance we have come from the early exclamation *all how true!* (6). Pope has brought his art into line with this sense of fresh commitment, laying aside the *flying stroke* or *wand'ring touch* which has characterized the earlier parts of the poem. He moves now to the general and representative rather than the particular and idiosyncratic. The ideal woman is Heaven's 'last best work' (272), something composed and achieved, like his own poem. And like his work it represents more than itself and finds a significance which is greater than the sum of its parts. The personal tribute at the end is Pope's opportunity to enrol himself among her virtues and to offer their relationship as the final validation:

> The gen'rous God, who Wit and Gold refines,
> And ripens Spirits as he ripens Mines,
> Kept Dross for Duchesses, the world shall know it,
> To you gave Sense, Good-humour, and a Poet.

(289–92)

11. *Epistle to Arbuthnot*

The opening lines of Pope's *Epistle to Arbuthnot* are dramatic, breathless and immediate:

> Shut, shut the door, good *John!* fatigu'd I said,
> Tye up the knocker, say I'm sick, I'm dead,
> The Dog-star rages! nay 'tis past a doubt,
> All *Bedlam*, or *Parnassus*, is let out:
> Fire in each eye, and Papers in each hand,
> They rave, recite, and madden round the land.

> (1–6)

Pope's poetry is full of individual people that he knew. It is also full of crowds – busy, anonymous and threatening. Here at the very start of the poem they are shut out, as though he cannot bear to confront the stupid rabble he had surveyed in *The Dunciad*. The door closes to secure his private world. Outside are the faceless mob of *Bedlam, or Parnassus*, the Bedlam lunatics or those who aspire to the heights of Mount Parnassus, the symbol of poetic aspiration. The ravings of madmen and the recitings of would-be poets are one and the same. Within the 'door' are Pope and his servant, John Searle, and his friend Dr John Arbuthnot, his physician and fellow Scriblerian. This opening, therefore, gives us a clue to one theme of the poem: Pope's desire to take stock of himself and his work. To do this he will examine his ideals as they have developed through his career and assess the importance for him of various relationships, those (so to speak) on the inside of the door and those on the outside.

In his 'Advertisement' prefixed to the poem, Pope refers to it as 'a Sort of Bill of Complaint, begun many years since, and drawn up by snatches, as the several Occasions offer'd'. Earlier versions of two passages had in fact already appeared in print (the 'Atticus' portrait in 1722, and lines 289–304 in 1732 as an imitation of Horace), and Pope had others by him in manuscript, ranging from a 260-line first-draft of a poem to another friend, William Cleland, to what was probably a miscellaneous collection of fragments compiled in response to the mounting personal attacks being directed at him in the wake of *The Dunciad* and the *Epistle to Burlington*. The epistle was assembled with some urgency because his old friend Arbuthnot was in his final illness (he died just over three weeks after publication), and indeed the poem develops a momentum and an emotional commitment that drives it through a whole range of tones. It is unified also by the theme of friendship itself.

Pope is not only alarmed and annoyed by invasions of his *physical* privacy ('They pierce my Thickets, thro' my Grot they glide', 8), but by the way they make demands on his opinions and emotions, those things which constitute a 'self'. Against this background, friendship is a powerful idea throughout the poem, friends being those people who help us to form a 'self' by their concern, encouragement and support. But as Pope says in *An Essay on Criticism*: 'Make use of ev'ry *Friend* – and ev'ry *Foe*' (214). In this poem we see how our enemies also help us, by being people we want to set ourselves against, to show how different we are from them. The poem is to this extent about friends *and* enemies, and out of the encounters Pope works at establishing a sense of his own identity, a self which he can measure against others and present to the reader with confidence. This helps us, I think, to get a sense of the unity and progression of a poem which can easily fall into separate set-pieces.

To begin with the friends. Arbuthnot himself is in a most direct way involved with Pope's life, and Pope means the first phrase literally:

> Friend to my Life, (which did you not prolong,
> The World had wanted many an idle Song)
> What *Drop* or *Nostrum* can this Plague remove?
> Or which must end me, a Fool's Wrath or Love?

> (27–30)

He toys with the idea of his friend's medicines being able to rid him of the *Plague* of those who pester him. The extremes of anger and love (one genuine, the other false) are both invalidated by being *a Fool's*. There is a lot of emotion playing around here, exaggeratedly misdirected and selfish. Set against this is the genial reassuring presence of Arbuthnot, the constant and trusted friend whose feelings are true. Arbuthnot is not, of course, silent. He is the 'interlocutor' (the figure the poet is conversing with), and was identified as such in the 1751 edition. Though he does not contribute much, what Pope gives him to say is strategically significant. When 'Pope' (I use inverted commas here to remind us that this is the 'Pope' projected by the poet) is warming to his task of railing against scribblers and is beginning to name names ('And has not *Colly* still his Lord, and Whore?/His Butchers *Henley*, his Free-masons *Moor*?', 97–8) the protective voice of Arbuthnot intervenes:

> Hold! for God-sake – you'll offend:
> No Names – be calm – learn Prudence of a Friend:
> I too could write, and I am twice as tall,
> But Foes like these!

(101–4)

'Arbuthnot' is of course being used tactically here. His prudent intervention allows Pope to get away with the rather crude and unfocused attack he has just made. After all, the *Whore* of Colley Cibber, the Poet Laureate, is an irrelevant side-swipe (Pope's satire is best, as we shall see, when it is focused relentlessly on the most appropriate facts and images). He is consciously building up to a climax of pent-up rage. Earlier satire has done no damage, or these people would not still be offending in the old ways. His frustration is part of his meaning, and Arbuthnot's interruption is an ingenious climax both emotionally and thematically. Pope builds on it by pressing on with a sudden change of tack as he in turn interrupts his friend:

> One Flatt'rer's worse than all;
> Of all mad Creatures, if the Learn'd are right,
> It is the Slaver kills, and not the Bite.

(104–6)

Suddenly there is a new perspective. The flatterer 'sucking up' (as we say) to his patrons and friends is imaged as a mad dog foaming at the mouth. The fawning *Slaver* is ultimately more harmful; this suggests that his own *bite* (which Colley Cibber, Henley and others have just felt) is both more dignified and healthy. In a poem about friendship it is important to be aware how flattery and mutual congratulation can sometimes pass for 'friendship', and to disentangle true commitment from empty politeness.

As well as Arbuthnot, the poem sets out a whole array of friends and genuine admirers, a roll-call that Pope is proud to make: Granville, Walsh, Garth, Congreve and others. Pope contrasts this with another list:

> From these the world will judge of Men and Books,
> Not from the *Burnets*, *Oldmixons*, and *Cooks*

(145–6)

The names (of writers whom Pope had considered had libelled him) are, we notice, plurals. They immediately become trivialized and miniaturized, not individuals with a character of their own, but representatives of

112

a race of undistinguished scribblers. In withholding from them a singular identity Pope lets them coalesce into a single malign race, a generic rather than an individual enemy.

We see how Pope is mapping out his relationships. His enemies tend to become pluralized as a swarm of troublesome creatures, while inside the door is individual friendship and a roll-call of admirers/friends:

> Happy my Studies, when by these approv'd!
> Happier their Author, when by these belov'd!
>
> (143–4)

The rhyme of *approv'd–belov'd* humanizes literary judgement and allows critical approval to warm into friendship, marking Pope's refusal to isolate literary achievement from human feeling. Friendship in *Epistle to Arbuthnot* is the seal on this relationship.

In the world of the scribbler, ideals of human community have been replaced by a negative kind of selfhood: bad writing and bad living are related:

> Who shames a Scribler? break one cobweb thro',
> He spins the slight, self-pleasing thread anew;
> Destroy his Fib, or Sophistry; in vain,
> The Creature's at his dirty work again;
> Thron'd in the Centre of his thin designs;
> Proud of a vast Extent of flimzy lines.
>
> (89–94)

Pope wonders at the sheer dogged persistence of the hack-writer who, undeterred by criticism, can produce an endless flow of verse almost by a spontaneous physical process. It is a powerful picture of the kind of self-absorbed creative fertility that horrified Pope. His selfhood as a poet is deliberately defined by a moral and social context. It is not 'self' placed in opposition to 'society', but is validated and expressed *through* the poet's chosen social group. Genuine selfhood for Pope is representative and responsible. The *self-pleasing* thread which the scribbler spins out of himself (like the spider spinning his sticky web from his own intestines) is the very opposite of the identity Pope constructs in this poem. The insect works at the *Centre*, but it is a centre with no reference to anything beyond. The flimsy tackiness around him does not achieve any firm or lasting relationship. The dirty threads are forever being re-made. If we set this against Pope's remark about his own poetic career ('No Duty broke, no Father dis-obey'd', 130) we see the contrast. The bonds of duty and respect are firm and lasting. They are no mere cobwebs to be

swept lightly away. We have already some idea, therefore, of the importance of relationships in this poem: friendship, community, responsibility,
duty – the bonds that hold firm.

The two full satirical portraits of the *Epistle* should be seen in this
context. They are individual studies which stand out from the background of faceless scribblers, and in method and character they are
consciously contrasted.

'Atticus' (lines 193–214) and 'Sporus' (305–33) are both men of power
at the centre of their worlds. 'Atticus' (Joseph Addison, 1672–1719) had
been during Pope's twenties the leader of literary taste, an influential
patron and pillar of the cultural establishment. Through the essays in his
periodical *The Spectator* (1711–12) Addison guided the taste of the age
in literature, manners, fashion and aesthetics, in a style which was to
prove a model to future generations for its poise, clarity, and above all,
urbanity. 'Urbanity' is a useful word which conveys exactly the sense of
someone living in an urban society (the opposite of a retreat to the
private and personal). The urbane manner which Addison cultivated
was the tone of a civilized man-of-affairs who was reasonable, self-
possessed and polite, and who could speak with assurance for his class
and his age. In other words, the Addisonian circle was uncomfortably
close to Pope's own ideal of a community of shared cultural values.
Indeed the younger Pope was for a time a protégé and admirer, but soon
came to resent Addison's rather aloof and patronizing nature. In the
context of the *Epistle to Arbuthnot*, where Pope is wanting to establish
his own cultural map and his place on it, his negotiation (a diplomatic,
urbane word!) with Addison and his admirers takes on a special significance. Where the spider/scribbler is *thron'd in the Centre* (93) Addison is
similarly seated, but in a place of public eminence where he will bear 'no
brother near the throne' (198). Addison's centre is his 'Senate'. It might
appear totally different from the spider's web, and yet the line 'And sit
attentive to his own applause' (210) conveys the idea that Addison is
feeding his own self-esteem rather than genuinely working for the public
good.

If Pope was to attack such a man (and an early version of Pope's
portrait was being circulated during Addison's lifetime), then a
battering-ram would be crude and ineffective. Addison could never be the
polar opposite of Pope himself. Instead, his principles and characteristics
had to be deftly and subtly differentiated, and to have maximum effect
something of Addison's own urbanity was necessary. This is what Pope

achieves in the portrait, first of all by the conjectural quality of his accusations ('were there One . . . Shou'd such a man . . . Who but must laugh, if . . . Who would not weep, if . . .'). The conditional phrasing is indirect but powerful. He is not turning to face Addison, but is talking behind his back to those who know and admire him. It is a wonderful snub. Pope worries out loud that the respected Addison may fit the picture he has drawn. Would it not be terrible *if* the great man were like this? Such indirectness brilliantly mimics what Pope sees as Addison's own character:

> Damn with faint praise, assent with civil leer,
> And without sneering, teach the rest to sneer;
> Willing to wound, and yet afraid to strike,
> Just hint a fault, and hesitate dislike;
> Alike reserv'd to blame, or to commend,
> A tim'rous foe, and a suspicious friend

(201–6)

So Pope is reaching back at Addison in the most appropriate way, via the friends through whom he indirectly operated. Addison's half-hearted politeness turns every positive into a negative. All is civil, faint, hesitating, reserved, timorous. Nothing is truthfully and directly expressed. In a poem which makes so much of friends and foes, the *tim'rous foe* and *suspicious friend* occupies an uneasy place. In Addison opposites meet, but not in a middle way which reconciles discordant elements (as with Martha Blount in *Epistle to a Lady*). These opposites slide into each other or circle around half-heartedly. There is no sense of direction or of any principle establishing itself. Much is summed up by the phrase *Willing to wound, and yet afraid to strike*: behind the tentativeness is a capacity to hurt, not by an honest, direct confrontation or a clean blow, but by something which injures more deeply. What Pope has succeeded in doing in this portrait is to wound Addison in much the same way.

The portrait of 'Sporus' (Lord Hervey, 1696–1743) is in a completely different vein. After the indirection and hesitation of the 'Atticus' passage, Pope will allow nothing to intervene in his relish for the task ahead. When Arbuthnot suggests that a fragile creature like Hervey should be handled delicately ('Who breaks a Butterfly upon a Wheel?', 308) Pope will have none of it:

> Yet let me flap this Bug with gilded wings,
> This painted Child of Dirt that stinks and stings

(309–10)

115

However, the joy will not be in squashing this insect, but in distending it into innumerable shapes and postures, playing with it and tormenting it ('mumbling of the Game they dare not bite', 314). The fun is not to crush Hervey with a single blow, but to keep him alive and to toy with the tormented object as it takes on a succession of grotesque forms:

> Eternal Smiles his Emptiness betray,
> As shallow streams run dimpling all the way.
> Whether in florid Impotence he speaks,
> And, as the Prompter breathes, the Puppet squeaks;
> Or at the Ear of *Eve*, familiar Toad,
> Half Froth, half Venom, spits himself abroad,
> In Puns, or Politicks, or Tales, or Lyes,
> Or Spite, or Smut, or Rymes, or Blasphemies.
> His Wit all see-saw between *that* and *this*,
> Now high, now low, now Master up, now Miss,
> And he himself one vile Antithesis.

(315–25)

It is Hervey's disconcerting doubleness that is emphasized, conveyed by Pope's holding up a kind of warped mirror which shifts and distorts his subject at every moment. Everything seems at first to be pouring out of Sporus's own mouth. The deadly *Slaver* (106) is nowhere more evident than here, transformed into a well-watered landscape (*shallow streams*) and then into the venom of a poisonous toad. With the word *spits* the verse itself seems to spit out a jumble of nouns in a torrent, until it reaches a climax in the triplet (lines 323–5) where the opposites of *that/this*, *high/low*, *Master/Miss* play *see-saw* until they climax in the concept of *Antithesis*, a word which achieves full emphasis rhythmically and logically. Pope dares to proclaim the utter appropriateness of his poetic technique. He is not attacking Hervey, he is *expressing* him.

With the word 'Amphibious' (326) we are taken back to the reptile world, and we suddenly recognize the figure who lies behind this passage. Satan in Milton's *Paradise Lost* is a shape-changer who metamorphoses into a toad and whispers a dream into Eve's ear. (We have seen the incident playfully used in Canto One of *The Rape of the Lock*. Here it is sinister and threatening.) This is the posture that Hervey is made to adopt as confidant of Queen Caroline ('Eve'). Milton had embodied Evil in a figure who could adopt any shape at will. Satan becomes, for example, a cormorant, and also a mist, allowing him to breathe his way into the serpent and speak through its mouth to tempt Eve. Pope goes on to make the parallel explicit:

> *Eve*'s Tempter thus the Rabbins have exprest,
> A Cherub's face, a Reptile all the rest;
> Beauty that shocks you, Parts that none will trust,
> Wit that can creep, and Pride that licks the dust.

(330–33)

Hervey is not, therefore, a harmless butterfly, but a source of evil: the devil himself, the shape-changer and father of lies and deception. Where Milton's Satan had remnants of his former angelic glory, we are allowed to glimpse Hervey's troubling beauty, but as something shocking. After all the gyrations he is finally, like the Satanic serpent, made to crawl on his belly and lick the dust.

With a supremely confident and daring change of tone Pope immediately switches the focus upon himself:

> Not Fortune's Worshipper, nor Fashion's Fool,
> Not Lucre's Madman, nor Ambition's Tool,
> Not proud, nor servile, be one Poet's praise
> That, if he pleas'd, he pleas'd by manly ways

(334–7)

After the ambiguities of Sporus (Hervey fathered his wife's eight children, but also had a male lover) Pope offers the alternative of his own integrity. The negatives build up in a series of dignified dismissals until we reach the crucial positive: *manly*. The de-humanized Sporus has made way for the poet to focus on his own humanity. His enemies are cheats and liars, while he is defined by human relationships (love, friendship, family):

> The distant Threats of Vengeance on his head,
> The Blow unfelt, the Tear he never shed;
> The Tale reviv'd, the Lye so oft o'erthrown;
> Th'imputed Trash, and Dulness not his own;
> The Morals blacken'd when the Writings scape;
> The libel'd Person, and the pictur'd Shape;
> Abuse on all he lov'd, or lov'd him, spread,
> A Friend in Exile, or a Father, dead

(348–55)

This is reminiscent of the poem's opening. Beyond the door which he has closed on his integrity is the crowd of undifferentiated enemies. Here they have disappeared, leaving only (with each half-line) a scar on his memory. But he manages to convey the idea that it is the human ideal that has been abused, and that he has been a martyr for a cause greater than himself.

117

This interlocking of the general and the personal is repeated as the epistle reaches its close. We encounter first the generalized 'good Man' (392–405), the embodiment of health, honesty, wisdom and truth, who knew 'No Language, but the Language of the Heart' (399) and who calls forth from the poet the simple statement: 'Oh grant me thus to live, and thus to die!' (404). Pope finds his ideal in a life well lived and well ended, and at this point his mind inevitably turns to two figures facing death: his aged mother (who died in 1733, after lines 406–19 had been written) and Dr Arbuthnot himself, who was seriously ill. It provides a melancholy but dignified ending and confirms the theme of how human relationships are the fullest expression of a person's humanity. This is conveyed rather startlingly when Pope pictures himself caring for his mother. By an extraordinary act of imaginative sympathy Pope takes on momentarily the identities of his parent *and* his friend, and himself becomes both the mother rocking the cradle and the doctor exercising his 'lenient Arts':

> Me, let the tender Office long engage
> To rock the Cradle of reposing Age,
> With lenient Arts extend a Mother's breath,
> Make Languor smile, and smooth the Bed of Death,
> Explore the Thought, explain the asking Eye,
> And keep a while one Parent from the Sky!

> (408–13)

Under the generalized picture is the intimate close-up of Pope smoothing out his mother's sheets and gazing into her face for a response. As a picture of human ties and commitments it makes the most effective contrast with those earlier chilling pictures, of Atticus enthroned in his 'little Senate' and Sporus in nasty intimacy 'at the Ear of *Eve*'. *Epistle to Arbuthnot* in the end asserts that the key to a person's worth lies in the quality of his personal relations, and that individual integrity is most surely expressed through friendship and love.

12. *Pope and Horace*

Between 1733 and 1738 Pope wrote and published eight imitations of the satires and epistles of Horace. We have already seen that the Roman poet was one of his models in writing the early *Essay on Criticism*. But whereas the influence of Horace's *Ars Poetica* on a work of that kind was almost unavoidable (even obligatory), Pope's decision in the 1730s to begin imitating some of Horace's best-known satires and epistles needs some explanation. Why should a poet of such creative energy and originality as Pope (he had already written the first *Dunciad*) turn in his full maturity as an artist to producing versions in English verse of poems from a far-off age about long-dead people? Were they merely an intellectual pastime (the poetic equivalent of a crossword puzzle)? Were they written just for the entertainment of a few friends who could appreciate such things?

In fact nothing could be further from the truth. The *Imitations of Horace* were directed at the heart of the cultural and political establishment, and Pope used them to express his most urgent concerns and his deepest principles. They are at the same time some of the most public and the most personal utterances he ever made as a poet. Writing about himself and his friends, he is also mounting an attack on the seat of power and the rotten, self-seeking, valueless society which it encourages.

According to Pope's later account to Joseph Spence, it was his friend Lord Bolingbroke who first suggested the enterprise to him. In January 1733, while visiting Pope (who was ill in bed) Bolingbroke saw a copy of Horace on the table, and in leafing through it his eyes lighted on the opening satire of Horace's second book. 'He observed' (Pope recalled) 'how well that would hit my case, if I were to imitate it in English. After he was gone, I read it over, translated it in a morning or two, and sent it to the press in a week or fortnight after. And this was the occasion of my imitating some other of the Satires and Epistles afterwards.'

In the outcry following the publication of the *Epistle to Burlington* Pope had been placed on the defensive. His new mode of polite epistolary satire, balancing a fervent idealism with a satirical thrust, the principles of his friends against others' misdirected energies, had been twisted from its purpose, and he himself was being attacked as an ungrateful and unprincipled opportunist. He had also just published a companion *Epistle*

119

to Bathurst which was in the same manner. Clearly some justification of his principles in these satirical-moral epistles was called for. He needed to reply to his critics with the voice of authority, to establish the tradition in which he was working, and perhaps find a respected ally who could support, and help him to express, his own ideals. This was the *case* that Horace *hit*. As Pope later announced in the Advertisement to the *Imitations* in his 1735 *Works*: 'The Occasion of publishing these *Imitations* was the Clamour raised on some of my *Epistles*. An Answer from *Horace* was both more full, and of more Dignity, than any I cou'd have made in my own person.'

Quintus Horatius Flaccus (65–8 BC) was, along with his slightly older contemporary Virgil, the great poet of Augustan Rome. He was favoured by the Emperor Augustus and was a protégé of the statesman Maecenas, who made him the gift of a country farm. Both of them encouraged and rewarded his writings, and both were addressed by him in his epistles. In reminding his contemporaries of the voice of Horace, therefore, Pope was implicitly comparing the Rome of Augustus Caesar with the Great Britain of George II (whose official name of George Augustus made the irony even greater). The enlightened culture of the one was set against the repressive regime of the other: Augustus against George Augustus, a Maecenas against a Walpole, and of course the patronage given to Horace against the opprobrium heaped on Pope. In the context of the 1730s, therefore, the act of imitating Horace could itself be a satirical tactic by encouraging the reader to weigh one society against the other, and we shall see in a moment some of the points Pope made out of this.

But as well as satirical contrasts, Pope was also able to develop parallels between Horace's characters and certain figures from his own age, flattering to those he admired, but embarrassing for others who found themselves illustrating the old Roman vices within the present day. Horace could be used in this way as a moral ally, an authority whose principles reflected Pope's own. This notion of a shared enterprise between Horace and himself is something that shines through all these *Imitations*, and just as Horace had looked back to his satiric predecessors to support his own methods, so Pope uses Horace to speak not just *for* him, but in a sense *with* him.

In the literary world of Pope's own day Horace was seen as embodying the art of genial conversation: a tone that was flexible, sprightly and engaging; a voice that never hectored or preached, but could alternate the sweet and the salty; a wit that made its point sharply and moved on; a seriousness that never became solemn; a manner that was easy and informal, while being shrewd and intelligent; above all a personality which was principled, moral and reliable, but also capable of a humorous self-deprecation. And overarching all these balanced ideas, the notion of balance itself, Horace's *modus in rebus* (measure in all things). The fact that such a combination of qualities has long been termed 'Horatian' is a tribute to Horace's ability to sustain this character through an enormous variety of topics and situations. But the concept of balance and moderation is misleading if it suggests a sameness of tone or lack of firm principles – it is only writers of passion who need to talk of balance, only those of compelling urgency who find moderation a bracing idea. And what is true for Horace is even more true for Pope.

In his *Satires* and *Epistles* Horace projects his own speaking voice as a sympathetic and persuasive character, a voice of authority and integrity whose point of view the reader willingly accepts. And behind the speaker we glimpse a kind of ideal rural existence, a viewpoint from which he can be intrigued, disturbed, perplexed or amused by the pageant of life beyond his boundaries. He can mingle with it and converse with it, but always in the background is the landscape of the simple unhurried life (Pope's garden and grotto function in a similar way). Horace's bounded landscape is his Sabine farm (the gift of his patron Maecenas) and his circle of friends who enjoy good food and engaging conversation. It embraces all who value the good life, which in Horace is a combination of the virtuous *and* enjoyable. Horatian 'pleasure' is a genuine contentment, contrasting with other men's frantic craving for worldly success or physical stimulation.

All these things Pope (who had read Horace closely since his youth and first translated him at about twelve years old) absorbed: the subtle play of wit, the flexible tone, the strenuous balancing of forces, a persuasive speaking voice capable of both intimacy and self-possession, a background landscape of personal integrity, and the intriguing interplay of the private and the public. These are infused not merely into the *Imitations* but elsewhere in his work (the *Epistles to Several Persons* and *Epistle to Arbuthnot*, for example). But one of the most important features of Pope's engagement with Horace is the way in which imitating him seems to have given Pope the confidence to develop a satirist-self, a voice which could assert or confess to the reader directly in the first person and act as a moral guide and touchstone.

For Horace, true freedom and contentment are to be found within the self. The moral life is, he says, 'that which will make you a friend to yourself', and elsewhere he asks: 'May I have what now is mine, or even

121

less, and live to myself'. This is literally a kind of self-possession. For him the best ethical guide is an inner voice which assesses and regulates our behaviour. Against this scrupulous integrity Horace opposes a negative image of selfhood: the relentless pursuit of money, status, sexual gratification and power. This is the self which is always in motion, always craving more, and never has time for doubt or scepticism, humour or friendship. Horace's satire works by setting in opposition these two notions of the self.

For Pope this distinction is of great importance, and it is one of the themes which his *Imitations of Horace* focus on. With Horace as his guide he has the confidence to set his own integrity against the world he judges. But it would be too simple to see this as Pope proclaiming his own virtue. In re-working Horace he uses the opportunity to take stock of himself and make a searching review of his own character as a poet and a man. After all, to present a 'self' so publicly to one's friends and enemies is a risky matter; it invites mockery and contradiction, and it also binds up the poet's life with his writings. It is in a sense putting himself on trial, and Horace is more circumspect and elusive than Pope on this count. We shall see that one of the interesting differences between Pope and Horace is the way the eighteenth-century poet more often declares his own character and principles. It seems as if Horace gave Pope the confidence to do this, but also made him feel that he had, in his satiric predecessor, something to live up to.

At the time Pope wrote, an 'imitation' was a recognized literary genre. The poet Dryden in 1680 had distinguished three kinds of translation, each with its own character: the *metaphrase* (word-for-word translation), the *paraphrase* (a freer version, but closely following the author's sense), and lastly the *imitation*: 'where the translator (if now he has not lost that name) assumes the liberty, not only to vary from the words and sense, but to forsake them both as he sees occasion; and taking only some general hints from the original, to run division on the groundwork, as he pleases.' This last phrase (a musical analogy) suggests that the imitator is improvising above the bass-line of the poet's tune. This is a helpful pointer to Pope's approach in the *Imitations of Horace*. We must bear in mind that the poems were published with Horace's Latin text on the facing page. This challenged the reader's skill in working through Pope's poem alongside the original. The delight lay in spotting the neat parallels the poet had found for the situations and characters in his original; but also (equally importantly) to see the points where Pope had departed from Horace, either by adjusting the emphasis or introducing a theme of his own.

The earliest of the imitations, that of the first satire in Horace's second book (*Satire* II.1), undertaken at Bolingbroke's suggestion, is a good example of the combination of parallelism and divergence which is the keynote of the 'imitation'. Horace's poem, a conversation with his friend Trebatius (an eminent lawyer), is a justification of the art of satire. His cautious, legally trained friend advises him against satire: it could run him into trouble with great men, and it upsets people; far better to write poems celebrating the triumphs of Caesar. That would gain him real rewards. Otherwise he'll end up in the lawcourts being sued for libel. Horace's response to this mealy-mouthed advice is to argue that satire is in his blood, and just as other people pursue their own favourite vices, so for him satire is an instinct: 'I *must* write.' To press his point home Horace turns to the earlier example of Gaius Lucilius (who had done more than anyone to establish a tradition of Roman satire). 'He it is I follow,' says Horace. Lucilius had stripped vice of its deceits and pretensions, but still kept the respect and friendship of great and good men. He was 'kind only to virtue and her friends', says Horace. Nor did this involve a compromise with his principles. In fact Lucilius was so honest that in his writings he revealed his most private self, as if he had copied it on to a votive tablet for public display.

Pope's handling of this poem can tell us a great deal. He keeps the basic outline, and the role of the nervous Trebatius is convincingly taken by his friend and legal adviser, William Fortescue (who had been Walpole's private secretary and was eventually to become Master of the Rolls). The choice between satire and panegyric is also the same, but while Horace rather modestly confesses he hasn't the strength for heroic verse, Pope oozes with disdain and satirically improvises the language of both patriotic epic and smooth flattery as if they were child's play.

But the most significant departure from his original is the dropping of Lucilius (the crux of Horace's argument about his satirical inheritance). Instead of recalling an ideal predecessor, Pope takes on the role himself. He speaks to us directly in a frank, confessional tone, acting out Horace's description of how Lucilius displayed the votive-tablet of his private self:

> I love to pour out all myself, as plain
> As downright *Shippen*, or as old *Montagne*.
> In them, as certain to be lov'd as seen,
> The Soul stood forth, nor kept a Thought within;
> In me what Spots (for Spots I have) appear,
> Will prove at least the Medium must be clear.

(51–6)

For the centrepiece of his imitation Pope singles out Horace's description of Lucilius: 'kind only to virtue and her friends'. He sets it out in capital letters as his own proclamation of principle, and offers it as a motto for *all* satirists (thus implying a satirical tradition running from Lucilius via Horace to himself):

> Hear this, and tremble! you, who 'scape the Laws.
> Yes, while I live, no rich or noble knave
> Shall walk the World, in credit, to his grave.
> TO VIRTUE ONLY and HER FRIENDS, A FRIEND
>
> (118–21)

In Pope's hands the phrase rings out like a warning, with a tone of menace quite different from the equivalent passage in Horace. But Pope goes further. Though he declares that 'Peace is my dear Delight' (75) we sense that he has most relish when his pen becomes a sword:

> What? arm'd for *Virtue* when I point the Pen,
> Brand the bold Front of shameless, guilty Men,
> Dash the proud Gamester in his gilded Car,
> Bare the mean Heart that lurks beneath a Star
>
> (105–8)

This is a fiercer tone than in the original, but again the key is Lucilius who (says Horace) 'tore the skin off' vice.

It seems that what Pope is doing here is identifying himself with both Lucilius *and* Horace. This tactic is evident when he comes to the passage describing Lucilius's private life. This is a translation of Horace's version:

When the courageous Scipio and the placid and wise Laelius withdrew into privacy from the crowded public stage, they would joke and sport with him at their ease while their vegetables were cooking.

Pope recognizes that embedded in these few lines is the old Horatian ideal of an off-duty retreat (simple food and honest friendship) which Horace has projected on to Lucilius. Pope therefore extends the passage along those lines, but substitutes instead a picture of his own private life, Horace-style, sitting in his grotto among his friends:

> The World beside may murmur, or commend.
> Know, all the distant Din that World can keep
> Rolls o'er my *Grotto*, and but sooths my Sleep.
> There, my Retreat the best Companions grace,
> Chiefs, out of War, and Statesmen, out of Place.
> There *St. John* mingles with my friendly Bowl,

The Feast of Reason and the Flow of Soul:
And He, whose Lightning pierc'd th' *Iberian* Lines,
Now, forms my Quincunx, and now ranks my Vines,
Or tames the Genius of the stubborn Plain,
Almost as quickly, as he conquer'd *Spain*.

(122–32)

Pope must have been delighted with his skill in creating out of his own life such a purely Horatian scene. He uses the satirical technique of incongruous apposition, but here to create a lightly humorous picture of his great friends, Lords Bolingbroke and Peterborough in their off-duty hours. The simple food becomes the food of the mind washed down with spiritual wine ('The Feast of Reason and the Flow of Soul'), the busy road to Hampton Court rolls over his head as he sits in his grotto, providing a rather comforting distant hum, and Lord Peterborough, the retired general, is faced mock-heroically with the 'stubborn Plain' of Pope's garden.

In redirecting passages like these towards his own life Pope intrudes himself more directly into his poem. A similar result occurs when he tackles the important lines where Horace talks of his birthplace. It was originally settled, he says, by frontiersmen sent to guard the borders against Rome's enemies. For Horace this symbolizes his position as both an outsider and a guardian of Rome's virtue, as well as humorously hinting that belligerence is in his blood. In imitating this passage Pope says nothing about his own ancestry or birthplace, but instead picks out the idea of the border and works his own variations on the theme. The result is a rather rueful picture of himself pursuing a Horatian middle way between extremes:

My Head and Heart thus flowing thro' my Quill,
Verse-man or Prose-man, term me which you will,
Papist or Protestant, or both between,
Like good *Erasmus* in an honest Mean,
In Moderation placing all my Glory,
While Tories call me Whig, and Whigs a Tory.

(63–8)

Pope stands more at the hub of things. He is not away at a distant frontier; the borderline *he* bestrides is the split between warring factions in religion and politics. He is not removed from events, but is a topic of controversy, a man discussed, pigeon-holed and labelled by others.

By centralizing his own opinions at moments like these, Pope places

125

himself under scrutiny. Where Horace pushes Lucilius forward as his model, Pope highlights his own life, friends and principles. This is not egotism, but a recognition of the intimate relationship between himself and his original. Pope in a way does not need a Lucilius, since his own 'model' is present in Horace's text. Where Horace had used Lucilius to defend the satirist's profession, Pope has the supportive voice of Horace speaking behind his own words, even at moments when we might think he has deserted his original.

Horace's *Satire* II.2 has for its context a typically Horatian occasion. The poet and his friends are about to go off and dine, when rather disconcertingly he stops them and delivers a discourse on the virtues of frugal living. The ideal, he says, is to be simple but not mean, and a simple life brings good health and energy. Even if you can afford luxury, you should spend your money on worthier things. To drive his point home Horace describes old Ofellus, his neighbour. Dispossessed of the farm he used to own, he now works as a tenant, and the poem ends with Ofellus's speech. He had always lived simply, and so Fortune cannot harm him now he is poor. It is not man, but nature who owns the land, and the person who drove him out will be displaced in his turn. All a man can do is bravely confront the blows of fate.

Pope's imitation of this poem is generally close, and he is particularly skilful at encapsulating Horace's argument in neat and simple pentameters (as though his style is reflecting the poem's message): 'To live on little with a chearful heart' (2), 'Between Excess and Famine lies a mean' (47), 'Now hear what blessings Temperance can bring' (67), and particularly the following couplet on his old friend Hugh Bethel (the poem's Ofellus):

> His equal mind I copy what I can,
> And as I love, would imitate the Man.

(131–2)

Such plain dignity (language reduced to its essentials) is exactly in tune with the poem's thought. But the homely Bethel, a man who enjoyed the simple, sociable life, is given only half of Ofellus's role. The most important part is again taken by Pope himself, who delivers the final speech in his own person. After all, the parallels were too neat to resist. As a Catholic he was penalized heavily and unable to inherit or purchase land, and his Twickenham villa was leased from his landlord Thomas Vernon. He could well feel that he knew how to face the vicissitudes of fortune. But just as Pope is beginning to sound solemn he introduces the voice of his friend Swift to lighten the tone:

> My lands are sold, my Father's house is gone;
> I'll hire another's, is not that my own . . .
> 'Pray heav'n it last! (cries Swift) as you go on;
> I wish to God this house had been your own:
> Pity! to build, without a son or wife:
> Why, you'll enjoy it only all your life.' —
> Well, if the Use be mine, can it concern one
> Whether the Name belong to Pope or Vernon?

(155–66)

This passage makes Pope's point very effectively. Little has changed, he suggests: tyranny and injustice are part of the human condition, and he uses the image to make a final declaration of his integrity:

> Let Lands and Houses have what Lords they will,
> Let Us be fix'd, and our own Masters still.

(179–80)

We realize that Pope is setting up a contrast between the way property moves from owner to owner and his own ideal of steadfastness, his determination to be his 'own master'. He can easily 'hire' another house, but no one will ever hire him. Pope's imitation, therefore, ends on a more positive note than his original, with the satirist declaring his fixed principles and his refusal to compromise them. Again we see how Horace allows Pope to find a voice (this time the Ofellus-voice) with which he can confront his own experiences.

Another ideal figure for Horace is his generous patron Maecenas, and in *Epistle* I.1 he addresses him directly. In writing to someone who was both a public statesman and a private friend Horace takes for his theme the contrast within himself between the life of action and the life of self-cultivation or, as he puts it, shaping himself to fit the world, or bending the world to himself. It is a life which shifts as regularly as the tide and like the rest of mankind he is an odd mixture of intellectual vigour and physical vulnerability. But he must make the best of himself and he relies on Maecenas as his guide and physician.

This is again a theme on which Pope can write with considerable personal feeling, and in choosing Lord Bolingbroke as his Maecenas, his 'Guide, Philosopher, and Friend' (177), Pope is making not just a personal commitment but a public declaration to the government that he is in the enemy camp. In other words, Pope takes up the 'public versus private' theme and sharpens the paradox by infusing it with his own situation and the extra ingredient of Bolingbroke – a man, not like Maecenas at the centre of power, but a recently exiled patriot robbed of his title and his political career. The ironies, therefore, are much greater. By the time Pope reaches the climax of Horace's epistle where the poet turns intimately to his friend, the way is open for a masterly re-working of his original. The tone suddenly warms into jocular informality and self-mockery. But with the words *my Guide, Philosopher, and Friend* the passage suddenly pivots back to the public man, the great figure of Bolingbroke waiting in the wings to oust a rotten government. The picture is presented as an inner ideal craved by Pope himself, what he wishes his friend would make out of *him* ('That Man divine whom Wisdom calls her own'). This sustained passage, which deserves to be quoted in full, remains close to Horace, but it actually seems to gain force from the Pope–Bolingbroke relationship to which it is being applied:

> You laugh, half Beau half Sloven if I stand,
> My Wig all powder, and all snuff my Band;
> You laugh, if Coat and Breeches strangely vary,
> White Gloves, and Linnen worthy Lady Mary!
> But when no Prelate's Lawn with Hair-shirt lin'd,
> Is half so incoherent as my Mind,
> When (each Opinion with the next at strife,
> One ebb and flow of follies all my Life)
> I plant, root up, I build, and then confound,
> Turn round to square, and square again to round;
> You never change one muscle of your face,
> You think this Madness but a common case,
> Nor once to Chanc'ry, nor to Hales apply;
> Yet hang your lip, to see a Seam awry!
> Careless how ill I with myself agree;
> Kind to my dress, my figure, not to Me.
> Is this my Guide, Philosopher, and Friend?
> This, He who loves me, and who ought to mend?
> Who ought to make me (what he can, or none,)
> That Man divine whom Wisdom calls her own,
> Great without Title, without Fortune bless'd,
> Rich ev'n when plunder'd, honour'd while oppress'd,
> Lov'd without youth, and follow'd without power,
> At home tho' exil'd, free, tho' in the Tower.

In short, that reas'ning, high, immortal Thing,
Just less than Jove, and much above a King,
Nay half in Heav'n – except (what's mighty odd)
A Fit of Vapours clouds this Demi-god.

(161–88)

The power of these lines lies in the way Pope moves from being awkward, modest and embarrassed, to being controlled, dignified and assertive; from the personal physical detail to the grandly generalized statement. In spite of what the poet says, there is a masterly *coherence* to the whole thing, evident in the capacity of the verse to adapt a similar pattern to convey the two extremes (*My Wig all powder, and all snuff my Band – Great without Title, without Fortune bless'd*). But the coherence is not won easily. When Pope is writing at his best (as he is here) there is often a tension between instability and order. Recalcitrant disordered material is given a temporary poise in the heroic couplet, as though Pope is striving to master these dissonant elements and make them cohere. And when, as here, it is infused with the tones of personal speech the effect can be rich and complex. Horace, like Pope, is a master of this sensitivity to tensions and tonal variations, and Pope must have learned a lot from his lifelong reading of the Roman poet.

A poem which still causes embarrassment to Pope's critics, editors and biographers is his *Sober Advice from Horace*, an imitation of Horace's *Satire* I.2. Until this century it was customary to omit the work from collected editions, and even today some scholars pass over it as quickly as possible, often with a remark about its being self-indulgent or unfunny or pornographic. In fact *Satire* I.2 represents a crucial element in Horace's output, and in deciding to imitate it Pope obviously wished to engage with a side of Horace that tended to be conveniently overlooked. Pope published it anonymously in rather grand style, once again with the Horatian Latin on the facing page, and he added an extra satirical dimension with some spoof footnotes from Horace's editor Richard Bentley (a leading character in *The Dunciad*) pointing out the Imitator's errors in the most smutty parts of the text. Pope did not publicly acknowledge the poem, commenting to a friend that it would appear 'a very indecent sermon, after the Essay on Man', but he must have recognized that this survey of mankind's ridiculous pursuit of sexual intrigue was packed with Horatian themes of human restlessness, vanity and self-deception:

> Hath not indulgent Nature spread a Feast,
> And giv'n enough for Man, enough for Beast?
> But Man corrupt, perverse in all his ways,
> In search of Vanities from Nature strays

(96–9)

Except for the substitution of contemporary examples, Pope's version of this satire remains close to the original. It begins with a panorama of human lewdness, the pathetic indignities of our search for sexual gratification. This is Fufidia the 'Self-Tormentor':

> Yet starves herself, so little her own Friend,
> And thirsts and hungers only at one End

(23–4)

And Sir Thomas Palmer the enthusiastic theatre-goer:

> To *Palmer*'s Bed no Actress comes amiss,
> He courts the whole *Personae Dramatis*

(71–2)

The pun on the word 'amiss' hits the point nicely, and Pope relishes the opportunity for introducing formal language (*Personae Dramatis*) into a context of undignified philandering. A similar technique is used in the following passage which mimics the formality of two pillars of the Church meeting under embarrassing circumstances:

> My Lord of *L*[ondon], chancing to remark
> A *noted Dean* much busy'd in the Park,
> 'Proceed (he cry'd) proceed, my Reverend Brother,
> 'Tis *Fornicatio simplex*, and no other:
> Better than lust for Boys, with *Pope* and *Turk*,
> Or others Spouses, like my Lord of [York]'

(39–44)

Politeness is strained but preserved, delicacy shades into euphemism (*My Lord, chancing to remark, A noted Dean, Reverend Brother, Proceed*), and hypocrisy seeps through in the way language denies the whole truth: 'lust for Boys' is suddenly monosyllabic and direct, where *Fornicatio simplex* dresses itself in academic dignity, as though lust becomes something else when practised by Latin scholars or Anglican clergymen.

The message of the poem is *serious*, though far from *solemn* (a vital distinction to make). In fact the satire plays amusing and thought-provoking games with Horatian themes, transposing them into physical terms. For example, 'that honest Part that rules us all' (87) becomes a sexual part, rather than head or heart; Horatian 'honesty' is still the standard, but here it is projected as frankness and plain-speaking; and 'Measure in all things' in this context means recommending an uncomplicated relationship with a willing partner:

> I'm a plain Man, whose Maxim is profest,
> 'The Thing at hand is of all Things the *best*,'
> But Her who will, and then will not comply,
> Whose Word is *If*, *Perhaps*, and *By-and-By*,
> Z—ds! let some Eunuch or Platonic take –
> So *B*[athurs]*t* cries, Philosopher and Rake!
> Who asks no more (right reasonable Peer)
> Than not to wait too long, nor pay too dear.

(153–60)

The *right reason* of his old friend Lord Bathurst neatly parodies the Platonic concept solemnly discussed by so many philosophers, and it signals that Pope is having fun with the materials of intellectual debate. To appreciate Horace and Pope fully we have to acknowledge that their ideals of *Nature*, *Sense*, *Reason*, and *solid Happiness* (all themes, we note, of *An Essay on Man*) are convictions vigorous enough to withstand a humorous application to sexual behaviour:

> Has Nature set no bounds to wild Desire?
> No Sense to guide, no Reason to enquire,
> What solid Happiness, what empty Pride?
> And what is best indulg'd, or best deny'd?

(143–6)

This last line recalls a repeated concern of Pope's: how to steer between indulgence and repression (see p. 149 below). *Sober Advice from Horace* supplies a context of human sexuality for this question. The poem itself refuses to repress, and its intelligent juggling with the great Horatian themes prevents it from sinking to indulgence. It is a disconcerting, smutty, swaggering and rather cocky piece of work, and any consideration of the 'Horatian' Pope which puts it embarrassingly to one side is not being true to the complexity of either poet.

In May and July 1738 Pope published two satirical dialogues called *One Thousand Seven Hundred and Thirty Eight*. They were not imitations of specific poems by Horace, but were billed as being '*something like* Horace' – dialogues, in other words, in the Horatian pattern, but forced by the state of things in 1738 to leave their genial Roman guide behind.

131

Critical Studies: Poetry of Alexander Pope

The title reads like an indictment of Pope's age, and indeed the two poems draw into the open much of the bitterness and political disgust that had been bubbling away beneath the earlier direct imitations of Horace. In 1740, perhaps with this in mind, they were re-named *Epilogue to the Satires.* In these companion dialogues the poet's disillusionment plays off against the naive and prudent 'friend' who tries to restrain him, and his indictment of Walpole and the establishment gathers considerable momentum. The second dialogue bristles with distaste and indignation, and in the exchange with the 'friend' Pope rejects nuance and subtlety to make a direct black-and-white declaration; the Horatian honest man has turned patriotic rebel:

> Ask you what Provocation I have had?
> The strong Antipathy of Good to Bad . . .
>   *Fr.* You're strangely proud.
>   *P.* So proud, I am no Slave:
> So impudent, I own myself no Knave:
> So odd, my Country's Ruin makes me grave.
> Yes, I am proud; I must be proud to see
> Men not afraid of God, afraid of me
>
>   (197–209)

It is through the first dialogue, however, that we can most clearly trace how much Pope is rooted in Horace, but also how his Roman model had at some point to be left behind. Near the beginning of the first dialogue the friend argues that Pope has not been observing the polite Horatian niceties:

> But *Horace*, Sir, was delicate, was nice;
> *Bubo* observes, he lash'd no sort of *Vice*:
> *Horace* would say, *Sir* Billy *serv'd the Crown,*
> Blunt *could do Bus'ness,* H—ggins *knew the Town,*
> In *Sappho* touch the *Failing of the Sex,*
> In rev'rend Bishops note some *small Neglects* . . .
> His sly, polite, insinuating stile
> Could please at Court, and make A U G U S T U S smile
>
>   (11–20)

Italics point up the euphemism and innuendo. But straining at the leash and against the time-serving advice of the friend (who tells him to 'Go see Sir R O B E R T') Pope moves in for the kill. In the course of the poem Pope releases a whole range of satiric tones, each of which hits its target in a different way. At one extreme is a combination of sorrow and disillusionment conveyed through intimate reminiscence:

> See Sir ROBERT! – hum –
> And never laugh – for all my life to come?
> Seen him I have, but in his happier hour
> Of Social Pleasure, ill-exchang'd for Pow'r;
> Seen him, uncumber'd with the Venal tribe,
> Smile without Art, and win without a Bribe . . .
> Come, come, at all I laugh He laughs, no doubt,
> The only diff 'rence is, I dare laugh out.
>
> (27–36)

It is said with a sense of personal betrayal, implying that Walpole has broken faith with himself and his friend. Though this is not taken from Horace, it powerfully evokes the Horatian ideal of the patron–poet relationship. Walpole here is a Maecenas who in the pursuit of power has compromised his integrity and his friendships.

The opposite but equally powerful extreme is the poem's visionary climax (closer than anything in the *Imitations of Horace* to the techniques of *The Dunciad*) where the spectacle of England's humiliation and disgrace passes before us in a parody of a street procession. Like the city pageants of Elkanah Settle it offers the spectator an allegorical interpretation, and Pope is there beside us pointing in horror. It is the triumphal march of Vice, pictured as the Whore of Babylon (with hints of Walpole's mistress, later wife, Molly Skerrett). The sacred has been ousted by the profane, and all moral standards (along with the flag) have been reversed:

> Lo! at the Wheels of her Triumphal Car,
> Old *England*'s Genius, rough with many a Scar,
> Dragg'd in the Dust! his Arms hang idly round,
> His Flag inverted trails along the ground!
> Our Youth, all liv'ry'd o'er with foreign Gold,
> Before her dance; behind her crawl the Old!
> See thronging Millions to the Pagod run,
> And offer Country, Parent, Wife, or Son!
> Hear her black Trumpet thro' the Land proclaim,
> That 'Not to be corrupted is the Shame.'
> In Soldier, Churchman, Patriot, Man in Pow'r,
> 'Tis Av'rice all, Ambition is no more!
> See, all our Nobles begging to be Slaves!
> See, all our Fools aspiring to be Knaves!
> The Wit of Cheats, the Courage of a Whore,
> Are what ten thousand envy and adore.
> All, all look up, with reverential Awe,

> On Crimes that scape, or triumph o'er the Law:
> While Truth, Worth, Wisdom, daily they decry –
> 'Nothing is Sacred now but Villany.'
>
> Yet may this Verse (if such a Verse remain)
> Show there was one who held it in disdain.

(151–72)

In its visionary fervour the passage is most un-Horatian, but in that final disdainful couplet we feel the disgust that Horace might have felt if transplanted to the world of *Seventeen Hundred and Thirty Eight*. The poem has travelled quite a distance from its opening, and from Horace, but that is the distance measured, Pope implies, by the decline of public morality.

13. *The Dunciad*

(i) The Growth of the Poem

It is appropriate that a poem about the insidious growth of a malign power should itself have grown in a menacing way. The history of the work's development from the three-book versions of 1728 and 1729 (with Lewis Theobald as the hero) to the final four-book *Dunciad* of 1743 (starring Colley Cibber) is a complicated one, but it shows how Pope regarded his poem as a document for the times, a work which lent itself to expansion and alteration as the social context changed. Furthermore, such an 'unstable' text which shifted and swelled from a small pamphlet to a heavy tome is a highly appropriate image for a work of 'Dulness', that insidious power which draws everything into its orbit and is forever shifting its ground.

Pope's onslaught on the hacks, academics, media-men, producers, pornographers and virtuosi of his day first appeared in the bookshops on 18 May 1728, an anonymous volume of less than sixty pages in a duodecimo format small enough to be slipped into the pocket. The title-page declared that it was printed in Dublin (untrue) and published by Anne Dodd (who always denied it). Clearly Pope was attempting to cover his tracks by suggesting the poem had been written by some Irish wit (perhaps even his friend Swift), and he substituted dashes for the individual names of the dunces, which allowed opportunists to publish various 'keys' to the poem's characters. Of course, all this was wonderful publicity, and on the day of its appearance, we are told, 'a Crowd of Authors besieg'd the Shop; Entreaties, Advices, Threats of Law, and Battery, nay Cries of Treason were all employ'd, to hinder the coming out of the *Dunciad*: On the other Side, the Booksellers and Hawkers made as great Efforts to procure it' (see Maynard Mack, *Alexander Pope. A Life*, p. 457).

By pretending that this first edition was an illicit one, Pope was then able in the following year to bring out the fully authorized version, his grand *Dunciad Variorum*. This bulky edition of 180 pages named names and was grotesquely padded-out with mock-learned footnotes and layers of prefatory material and appendices. It must have been a very satisfying joke for him to see his surreptitious little volume transformed within a twelvemonth into a burlesque 'classic'.

The 1729 version of the poem is in three books (containing the material covered in books I–III of the 1743 version) and has for its hero the dramatist and editor, Lewis Theobald, who is seen in his library sacrificing his works to the goddess Dulness, is visited by her, chosen as her new monarch, enthroned, entertained with ridiculous games, and in the third book is granted a prophetic dream by his predecessor Elkanah Settle which climaxes in a vision of the return of universal darkness. This text (which can claim to be more consistent and unified than the final version) is the culmination of Pope's original intention for his poem.

But if Pope's enemies thought they could rest in peace they were to be mistaken. In 1742 appeared *The New Dunciad: As it was Found in the Year 1741. With the Illustrations of Scriblerus, and Notes Variorum*, a thoroughly annotated edition of a poem which showed the fulfilment of Settle's prophecies about the triumph of Dulness. It describes the triumphant progress of the goddess and her establishment of 'the Kingdom of the Dull upon earth'.

Out of these two texts Pope assembled the single poem we now read as *The Dunciad*. The 1742 *New Dunciad* became the long fourth book, and the original apocalyptic ending again concluded the whole, only this time not as part of the hero's vision, but as a universal disaster extinguishing also the poet himself. Pope made many subtle changes to the original three books, but the most momentous innovation was his replacement of Theobald as the epic's hero by the far more controversial figure of Colley Cibber, the Poet Laureate. In this daring manoeuvre there were gains as well as losses.

Lewis Theobald (1688–1744) was a particularly appropriate hero for the first *Dunciad*, since his career unusually combined several of the attributes of Dulness. In his twenties he made a minor name for himself as a poet, and his odd and rather amusing poem *The Cave of Poverty* (1714) explored a dark, lurid world of the imagination and was a direct influence on the setting and imagery of Pope's poem. In his thirties Theobald actually collaborated with Elkanah Settle on some extravagant theatrical works, and by 1725 was himself writing successful pantomimes for the London stage which made spectacular use of stage effects and machinery. But there was another side to Theobald: he was a knowledgeable and astute Shakespeare scholar. Pope was especially galled by his *Shakespeare Restored: Or A Specimen of the Many Errors as well Committed as Unamended by Mr Pope in his late Edition of this Poet* (1726).

Theobald knew the old Shakespeare editions well (and Pope himself incorporated some of his corrections into his second edition), but his tone was patronizing and his finnicky preciseness was alien to Pope's more urbane approach to Shakespeare. Enshrining 'pidling *Tibalds*' (*Epistle to Arbuthnot*, 164) as the hero of *The Dunciad* allowed Pope to fuse a variety of appropriate settings (the Cave of Poverty, the Pantomime-theatre, the book-lined study), establish a credible line of descent (through the old city-poet Settle to his young collaborator Theobald), and turn his own poem into a text conscientiously edited in Theobald-style. Even the final 1743 version of *The Dunciad* is clearly marked by the odd variety of interests that Theobald's career covered.

By 1743, however, Theobald was respectable (he had produced his own authoritative edition of Shakespeare in 1734), uncontroversial, long retired from his extravagant theatrical ventures, and Pope's grudge had probably grown less. But at this time another figure, eminent throughout the literary world as the embodiment of comic pomposity, found himself uncomfortably in Pope's sights. Colley Cibber (1671–1757) was in many ways a rather endearing character. A professional actor since 1690, he had made his reputation in eccentric comic roles, had written several highly successful comedies and had entered theatrical management. But in 1730 he was drawn into unsuitable territory when he defeated Lewis Theobald for the appointment as Poet Laureate. The dignity and demands of the office hardly suited him, and he became increasingly the butt of satire. This became worse with the publication of his autobiography (*An Apology for the Life of Colley Cibber, Comedian*, 1740), an engaging, anecdotal work marred by endless self-justification.

In his relations with Pope, Cibber probably had every right to feel hard done by. In 1735 Pope out of the blue included a biting line in *Epistle to Arbuthnot*: 'And has not *Colly* still his Lord, and Whore?' (97). Cibber ignored this, and in his *Apology* was polite and conciliatory. But to find himself the hero of the *New Dunciad* (1742) was too much, and he at once published a *Letter from Mr Cibber to Mr Pope*. 'I believe I know more of *your* whoring than you do of *mine*,' he remarked, and proceeded to retail an anecdote of an occasion when he discovered Pope in a brothel in a far from dignified posture. The literary world was delighted. Prints began to appear graphically illustrating the incident, and Pope must have felt more than ever the weight of his physical deformities.

The anecdote may have been founded on an actual incident; but whatever the case it was the greatest impetus for Pope to replace Theobald with Cibber for the revised four-book *Dunciad* of 1743. As a hero, Cibber is particularly valuable to Pope by virtue of being Poet Laureate. His role as the official royal poet raises his significance and genuinely involves the fate of Britain's national culture with the antics of the hero. It also places him in a tradition (descending from Jonson and Dryden) where he could hardly avoid being seen as a burlesque figure. The poem's atmosphere of jovial but misdirected energy is highly suitable to Cibber's character, and his pride and self-obsession fit him beautifully into the mould of Dulness.

There are, however, inevitable awkwardnesses. Cibber was totally detached from the world of dusty academic scholarship and editing (such powerful images in the poem, both text and footnotes), and Theobald's 'Gothic Library' is rather incongruous for him. Nor was Cibber poor ('Swearing and supperless' has less sting than it had for Theobald). Also, importantly, Cibber did not like pantomime and had no direct connection with the work of Elkanah Settle, so that a crucial link in the dunce-inheritance is missing. Nevertheless, the mock-heroic presence of King Colley, the pompous Poet Laureate, is what gives the final version of the poem its characteristic flavour, and whatever awkwardnesses there may be, we are the richer by having (and still reading) both the three-book and four-book *Dunciads*.

(ii) A Commentary on the 1743 *Dunciad*

The action of the four-book *Dunciad* of 1743 begins in the 'Cave of Poverty and Poetry', a remote cell somewhere near Bedlam, the hospital for the insane (i, 29). It is an empty, draughty place, and the phrase 'Music caus'd by Emptiness' (i, 36) is the first of several references in the poem to flatulence and to images of speech breaking down into sound and air (brayings, hissings and rumblings). Here it suggests that, like the Cave of Spleen in *The Rape of the Lock*, this is a place within the human body, that Dulness's seat is inside all of us. In the first of many shifts of scale the cave becomes a kind of magician's hat, out of which emerge monstrous forms of poets and their endless printed works, the pulp publishing that serves to produce only waste-paper. It is the magic spring of dunce-literature which will never run dry. Here the goddess Dulness sits enthroned, and the cave now expands to become the original Chaos, that sea of all potential matter which begins to stir beneath her gaze. 'Nameless Somethings' (i, 56) take shape, and we soon understand that this chaotic world is like the dunce-poet's brain as ideas for a new work start to form. But in this confused mind everything joins up wrongly: images are incongruous, metaphors become entangled, genres mix together, and as we watch, a scene gradually assembles (as though the poet's work is taking shape before us) and we find ourselves in a theatre watching an extravagant spectacle, with the moveable scenery hilariously jumbled. Fruits hang across an icy landscape and a desert scene is decorated with flowers:

> Here gay Description Ægypt glads with show'rs,
> Or gives to Zembla fruits, to Barca flow'rs;
> Glitt'ring with ice here hoary hills are seen,
> There painted vallies of eternal green
>
> (i, 73–6)

This jumbled pantomime-stage is a projection of the dunce-poet's brain. Queen Dulness herself is present in the royal box swathing the whole spectacle in dry ice and projecting her fools-colours over them. She is at the same time the pop-star, the stage manager and the audience of her own production, and greets it with ecstatic 'self-applause' (i, 82).

The sustained passage I have just described (i, 55–84) is a masterly example of Pope's fluid technique throughout *The Dunciad*. The scene is both an internal and an external one. Images in the brain are projected on to an exterior scene, and the description of events and locations in turn mimics the fluidity of ideas as they pass through the mind. It is a daring procedure on Pope's part and risks sinking into the morass of confusion he is aiming to capture. What prevents him from doing this is his artistic control of the kaleidoscopic picture, his awareness of the cultural implications of Dulness, and above all his infinitely resourceful language.

With the next paragraph we find ourselves at a specific event, the Lord Mayor's Day procession through the City of London, and in particular the investiture of Sir George Thorold as Lord Mayor in November 1719. As the printed note says: 'This important point of time our Poet has chosen, as the Crisis of the Kingdom of *Dulness*, who thereupon decrees to remove her imperial seat from the City, and overspread the other parts of the Town . . .' It is a characteristically dunce-like occasion, a mixture of empty pomp and mass entertainment, the day when by tradition the city magnates paraded in their finery through the streets along with a procession of decorated chariots. The City Poet (at this time Elkanah Settle) exercised his ingenuity in creating the visual symbolism and the pageant's crude speeches, and the day was rounded off with a feast for the dignitaries and fireworks for the masses, who gaped open-mouthed at the glittering display.

However, the Lord Mayor's Day itself is not the focus for attack. It is seen as a symptom and a symbol of something greater. The 'City' was where, as now, the real power in society lay, among the profiteers, stock-jobbers and middle-men. It was they who supported the Prime Minister (Walpole), and the weapon of this pro-government establishment was the network of journalists, popularizers, entrepreneurs, newspaper owners and publishers, all of whom served in their different ways to sustain the Prime Minister's power-base. The enemy of any such entrenched group is a culture which informs, educates and humanizes (that culture to which Pope and his friends considered they belonged), and the establishment's ally is mass entertainment, pulp journalism, soft pornography, spectaculars – anything that settles the public mind into passivity, absorbs its energies and lulls it into complacency. By beginning his work with the Lord Mayor's Day procession, therefore, Pope is homing in on the power-base of Dulness and is giving his poem on the collapse of culture a cutting political edge.

The goddess contemplates the scene, now quiet at the close of day. While mayors and sheriffs dream about their triumphs and hack-poets work sleeplessly in their garrets, she recalls how the City Poets have served her cause since Elizabethan times ('In each she marks her Image full exprest', i, 107) and how her power has spread to the Poet Laureate (named 'Bays' because of the crown of bay laurel traditionally worn as a mark of public honour). Colley Cibber is extending her influence to both 'Stage and Town' (i, 109, the 'Town' being the smart western areas of London, very different from the 'City'), and it is this figure who begins to take shape before us under Dulness's gaze. Cibber, soon to be singled out for his greatest role as hero of Pope's epic, sits in despair amid a chaos of his own making, innumerable discarded scribblings and the remnants of authors whose works he has plundered. His bookshelves bend under the weight of his 'Gothic Library' (reminding us that the term 'Gothic' had overtones of anti-civilization) containing none of the works of classical Greece or Rome. These ranks of heavily bound books turn his room into a catacomb with shelves of preserved corpses ('Mummies', 'Dry Bodies'), and this scene develops pagan implications as he erects an altar of twelve massive volumes and prepares a public sacrifice ('hecatomb') in honour of the goddess.

It is clear from his address to her (i, 163–224) that he regards Dulness as a protective power, in the special sense of shielding him from intellectual challenge. By spreading her mists of mediocrity she will secure his position among authors:

> O! ever gracious to perplex'd mankind,
> Still spread a healing mist before the mind;
> And lest we err by Wit's wild dancing light,
> Secure us kindly in our native night.
>
> (i, 173–6)

Cibber contemplates his career as actor, dramatist and poet, seeing himself as the preserver of the government – though only on the level of the geese whose cackling saved Rome from attack. At the heart of this parody-saviour of the state is an inordinate pride rooted in self:

> What then remains? Ourself. Still, still remain
> Cibberian forehead, and Cibberian brain.
>
> (i, 217–18)

This is delightfully self-absorbed, and no one can quarrel with the adjective *Cibberian* which Pope must have hoped would enter the language. The Poet Laureate's dedication to Dulness is above all a devotion to himself.

Cibber now addresses his works as his own children, the result of illicit 'liaisons' with other authors, or unbound works which he sees as innocent souls not yet encased in flesh. He considers the degrading fate of all those printed sheets and the indignities they have to go through. (In Book II Pope himself will contribute to this degradation.) The best he can hope for is that they will remain in limbo as part of the chaotic seedbed that Dulness knows so well:

> Soon to that mass of Nonsense to return,
> Where things destroy'd are swept to things unborn.
>
> (i, 241–2)

He lights the pyre and flames consume his works. The sudden illumination wakes the slumbering goddess who has nodded off over the poem *Thule* by Ambrose Philips, one of Pope's favourite butts. Seizing this only available paper she swirls into Cibber's room and extinguishes the fire, filling the place with her presence like a genie released from a bottle. She is a figure of inspiration able to breathe into her worshippers and their works, and her foggy figure dilates awesomely. In an instant she transports Cibber to the cave, her 'sacred Dome' (i, 265) which he immediately recognizes as home, full of the fragments and odd hybrids of texts that he can appreciate.

141

Dulness anoints him with her drug, and a monstrous parody of an owl (the traditional bird of wisdom) perches on his head, turning him into an emblem of folly. She proclaims Cibber her representative at Court ('Lift up your gates, ye Princes, see him come!', i, 301) and looks to the day when the King himself will be in her power; she will nurse him like a child and rock the throne as if it were a cradle. The role of parody-mother is characteristic of Dulness: she automatically transforms her followers to children, comforts them by pandering to their desires and insulates them from intellectual or moral challenge. As she ends her speech, the choir of the Chapel Royal joins forces in song as if performing one of his own laureate odes, and in a parody of the royal coronation, 'God save King Colley' reverberates round London, its dying echo (typically in this burlesque poem) becomes the cry of 'Coll!' in the butchers' shops. But the book ends with a lower plunge into the mud, with the croak of the frogs as they welcome the great log they have accepted as their king.

At the beginning of Book Two, Cibber is installed 'high on a gorgeous seat', a position of eminence recalling the opening lines of Book Two of Milton's *Paradise Lost*, where Satan sits 'high on a throne of royal state'. The atmosphere of Milton's Hell lies behind the world of Pope's *Dunciad*, with Cibber enthroned satanically as an 'Antichrist of wit' (ii, 16), and these implications grow stronger as the poem develops. After the complexities of Book One, Book Two is clearer in its action, and clearer too are the allusions to the material of classical epic.

To celebrate Cibber's rule over the literary world Dulness proclaims her 'high heroic Games' (ii, 18), a series of activities symbolizing the nastiness and pointlessness of the sub-literary world. In Book Twenty-Three of Homer's *Iliad* Achilles had held funeral games for his dead friend Patroclus: a chariot-race, boxing, wrestling, foot-racing, hand-to-hand combat, discus-throwing and archery, and the episode was closely copied by Virgil in Book Five of his *Aeneid*. Both epics present the foot-race as comic. In Homer Ajax is in the lead when Ulysses calls for help to the goddess Pallas:

> Assist O Goddess! (thus in Thought he pray'd)
> And present at his Thought, descends the Maid.
> Buoy'd by her heav'nly Force, he seems to swim,
> And feels a Pinion lifting ev'ry Limb.
>
> (Pope's translation, *Iliad*, xxiii, 901–4)

Pallas also ensures that Ajax slips on the 'slimy Dung' (the remains of an earlier sacrifice):

> Besmear'd with Filth, and blotted o'er with Clay,
> Obscene to sight, the ruefull Racer lay . . .
> Thus sow'rly wail'd he, sputt'ring Dirt and Gore;
> A burst of Laughter echo'd thro' the Shore.
>
> (xxiii, 911–22)

Similar antics occur in the *Aeneid* (v, 315–47) when Nisus slips on a puddle of 'Holy Gore' (Dryden's translation) and reaches out to trip another runner so that his friend will win.

I have gone into some detail on this point because it is a representative example of the many epic incidents throughout *The Dunciad*. In the inaugural event of Pope's games the publishers Lintot and Curll race each other for the phantom poet. The unscrupulous Curll slips on the dirty material which Corinna has deposited near his shop ('the plash his wickedness had laid', ii, 76). This alludes to Curll's procuring of some of Pope's youthful letters which he then published. (Curll, in other words, is up-ended in his own filth.) In Pope's race it is the victim who calls for divine aid, and in a daring parody of a petition to the gods, Curll's prayer reaches Jove's orifice and he wins the race in spite of his 'brown dishonours' (ii, 108). It is worth remembering that classical epic has its lighthearted moments, and that Pope is here developing an episode of less than heroic dignity. The dirty element has a 'sympathetic force' (ii, 103) appropriate to the victor. Needless to say, the immodest Curll also wins the pissing game (ii, 157–90) symbolic of the dirty tricks practised by competitive booksellers.

The wealthy patron arrives for a tickling session and the poets allow their wit to be debased to shameless flattery, an activity which Pope sees as an unsettling mutual manipulation (Latin *manus* = 'hand'):

> While thus each hand promotes the pleasing pain,
> And quick sensations skip from vein to vein
>
> (ii, 211–12)

After this straining for poetic ecstasy the dunces compete in sheer noise, allowing Pope to create some sonorous effects of his own ('And Noise and Norton, Brangling and Breval,/Dennis and Dissonance . . .', ii, 238–9) where the alliteration drains the names of any meaning but the sound.

Dulness now summons her followers to Fleet Ditch, the notorious open sewer and assembly-point for the City's filth. Like mindless children the party hacks and unscrupulous slanderers plunge into the media (their natural element) and each is characterized by the motions he makes in the yielding material. The victor is Smedley, so long immersed that the underworld seemed to him a landscape of the imagination, 'wafting Vapours from the Land of dreams' (ii, 340). Taking turds for mud-nymphs, he clearly relishes his occupation, and as Pope coyly notes: 'The Allegory evidently demands a person dipp'd in scandal, and deeply immers'd in dirty work' (note to ii, 291).

To close the games a 'gentler exercise' is prescribed: the challenge to remain awake during a reading of the works of Henley (the religious orator) and Blackmore (the writer of ponderous epics of King Arthur). The clerks 'thro' the long, heavy, painful page drawl on' (ii, 388) and the influence of Dulness spreads in a slow-motion burlesque of religious hysteria:

> What Dulness dropt among her sons imprest
> Like motion from one circle to the rest;
> So from the mid-most the nutation spreads
> Round and more round, o'er all the sea of heads.

> (ii, 407–10)

Nutation is a nodding of the head (Latin *nutare*), but also a slight oscillation of the earth's axis recently described by astronomers; so that in one word Pope beautifully combines an immediate physical sensation with the cosmic implications of the spread of Dulness in preparation for his apocalyptic climax.

After the celebratory games comes, in Book Three, Cibber's initiation into the secret knowledge of Dulness. His mother-substitute cradles him in her lap (an emblem of his servitude to her) and she induces a slumber which carries him off into a world of dream-vision where he can view past, present and future and understand the nature of his own task. Down in the nether regions he encounters the figure of Elkanah Settle, who is to be his guide and mentor, and whose work for Dulness he is to continue. In Book Eleven of Homer's *Odyssey* Ulysses had told how he descended into the underworld and talked with the ghosts of the Trojan heroes. In Virgil's *Aeneid* Book Six the sibyl led Aeneas down to Hell where his dead father showed him the heroic race who were to be his descendants. And in Milton's *Paradise Lost* the Archangel Michael led Adam to a lofty hill and revealed to him the future course of history and the fate of his successors. It was obviously necessary for *The Dunciad* to have a revelatory episode of this kind, and Pope handles it with assurance, re-working its traditional motifs of the unfolding of history, the inheritance of power or responsibility, and moments of recognition and wonder.

Settle leads Cibber up a hill (which is predictably clouded) and his eyes are drawn to the distant reaches of the world, to the boundaries of civilization which bred the Gothic hordes and 'clouds of Vandals' (iii, 86) who overran the Roman empire. With relish Settle sketches a picture of 'streets pav'd with Heroes, Tyber choak'd with Gods' (iii, 108), and his language itself becomes choked as he contemplates monastic Britain:

> Men bearded, bald, cowl'd, uncowl'd, shod, unshod,
> Peel'd, patch'd, and pyebald, linsey-wolsey brothers
>
> (iii, 114–15)

Britain is the 'fav'rite Isle', and Settle conjures successive scenes of Dulness's progeny 'as they rise to light' (iii, 130), beginning with Cibber's own son, Theophilus (who had followed his father on to the stage and was making a name as an actor-manager and dramatist), through various political hacks, the critics Dennis and Gildon, to two contrasting figures, Leonard Welsted and Thomas Hearne. Welsted, a poet and translator of Longinus's treatise on the Sublime, is gracefully addressed in lines which are a delicious parody of one of the most famous passages (at that time) of English poetry. Sir John Denham's poem *Cooper's Hill* (1642) had invoked the River Thames in terms which were thought to express the eighteenth century's poetic ideal:

> O could I flow like thee! and make thy stream
> My great example, as it is my theme;
> Tho' deep, yet clear; tho' gentle, yet not dull;
> Strong, without rage; without o'erflowing, full.

In Pope's hands Welsted becomes the exact reverse. The lines retain Denham's poise and smoothness, but the terms (and the liquid) have changed:

> 'Flow Welsted, flow! like thine inspirer, Beer,
> Tho' stale, not ripe; tho' thin, yet never clear;
> So sweetly mawkish, and so smoothly dull;
> Heady, not strong; o'erflowing, tho' not full.
>
> (iii, 169–72)

A very different style is called for when the scene shifts to a dusty room in St Edmund Hall, Oxford, where Thomas Hearne ('Wormius') is engrossed in one of his scholarly editions of medieval history. Pope regarded him as a quaint anachronism, and the conversation slips into a mock-medieval language reminiscent of Spenser's *Faerie Queene*:

> 'But who is he, in closet close y-pent,
> Of sober face, with learned dust besprent?'
> 'Right well mine eyes arede the myster wight,
> On parchment scraps y-fed, and Wormius hight.'

(iii, 185–8)

Pope takes an obvious pride in the language he lavishes on his dunces, as though the final insult is the care with which he awards them an appropriate, 'decorous' style. It is an extra twist of the knife, but it also preserves Pope's own genius above the base material in which he is working.

Settle warms to his task and introduces his 'son' to the new world which is about to be created. A model for the kind of apocalyptic rebirth which Dulness will bring about is offered by the theatre, and the extravagant pantomimes or harlequinades which were enormously successful during the 1720s, and which were threatening, along with Italian opera, to drive legitimate drama from the stage:

> [He] look'd, and saw a sable Sorc'rer rise,
> Swift to whose hand a winged volume flies:
> All sudden, Gorgons hiss, and Dragons glare,
> And ten-horned fiends and Giants rush to war.
> Hell rises, Heav'n descends, and dance on Earth:
> Gods, imps, and monsters, music, rage, and mirth,
> A fire, a jigg, a battle, and a ball,
> 'Till one wide Conflagration swallows all.
>   Thence a new world, to Nature's laws unknown,
> Breaks out refulgent, with a heav'n its own:
> Another Cynthia her new journey runs,
> And other planets circle other suns.
> The forests dance, the rivers upward rise,
> Whales sport in woods, and dolphins in the skies

(iii, 233–46)

Pope has in mind productions such as Lewis Theobald's *Harlequin Sorcerer* or his *The Rape of Proserpine* (both 1725) in which (says Pope in a note to line 237) 'This monstrous absurdity was actually represented'. In fact a stage direction from *The Rape of Proserpine* reads as follows: 'An Earthquake is felt, and part of the Building falls; and through the

Ruins of the fall'n Palace Mount *Aetna* appears, and emits Flames. Beneath, a Giant is seen to rise, but is dash'd to pieces by a Thunderbolt hurl'd from *Jupiter*.' The action continues with Pluto seizing Proserpine and carrying her off in his chariot. His mother Ceres then descends and in her anger sets fire to a field of corn (Pope recalls this in his note to iii, 312). From under the stage an infernal voice proclaims: 'Let universal Order die!'

Scenes like these from Theobald's pantomime lie behind much of the extravagant activity of *The Dunciad*, where Nature's laws are suspended, weird transformations occur, and universal order finally *does* die. John Rich (a theatre-manager who led the fashion for these media events) appears as a pantomime 'Angel of Dulness' (iii, 257) working the thunder-machine and causing the sun and stars to move according to his will, a role which establishes him as the parody-deity of this anti-Newtonian theatrical universe.

Settle nostalgically recalls how he himself had once led the way in spectaculars of all kinds: operatic entertainments, masques, the Lord Mayor's Day procession, and (a sensitive issue for Pope!) the annual Pope-burning pageant (the predecessor of Guy Fawkes Night):

> Tho' long my Party built on me their hopes,
> For writing Pamphlets, and for roasting Popes

(iii, 283–4)

Settle foresees how under the guidance of Dulness and her chosen monarch Cibber the civilized world will become a giant theatre where fantasies of every kind will be played out. Each individual will be licensed to 'do his own thing' and in defiance of any principles of order, nature, reason, good sense or propriety, everyone will have a glorious time.

The long fourth book declares 'the Completion of the Prophecies', and Pope begins it with a personal plea, that as the endless night of Dulness approaches he may be allowed a last 'dim Ray of Light' (iv, 1) by which to complete his poem amidst the encroaching 'darkness visible' (iv, 3), a phrase which takes us back to Milton's Hell:

> from those flames
> No light, but rather darkness visible
> Served only to discover sights of woe,
> Regions of sorrow, doleful shades, where peace
> And rest can never dwell

(*Paradise Lost*, i, 62–6)

147

Dulness mounts her throne, and under her stool lie her groaning victims: science, wit, logic, rhetoric, morality and the Muses, tortured, exiled or murdered. Tyranny's new order is represented by a figure from Italian opera who trips on in her motley garments and delivers a 'Recitative' boasting of her vocal gymnastics. She demands that the great composer Handel (who had abandoned Italian opera for English devotional oratorio) be arrested, and Dulness duly banishes him.

In response to an apocalyptic fart, the innumerable dunces swarm around their Queen, surrendering themselves to the overpowering force of the vortex. Out of the crowd the poet begins to distinguish individual figures: the familiar milky face of Lord Hervey ('Narcissus') and Sir Thomas Hanmer ('Montalto') bearing a presentation copy of his prestigious Oxford edition of Shakespeare. Dulness uses this opportunity to announce her principles of editing: substitute as many of your own words as possible for 'errors' in the text, and thoroughly re-write and 'correct' your original:

> 'Leave not a foot of verse, a foot of stone,
> A Page, a Grave, that they can call their own;
> But spread, my sons, your glory thin or thick,
> On passive paper, or on solid brick.

(iv, 127–30)

It is one of the principles of Dulness that material values are all that matter; writing is a trade as practical and adaptable as bricklaying (and equally subject to the laws of supply and demand).

The great figures begin to assemble. Dr Richard Busby, Headmaster of Westminster School and famous for his strict regime, is presented as the repressive educator who implants dead knowledge as a discipline and hangs a 'jingling padlock on the mind' (iv, 162). In response Dulness thinks nostalgically of the days of James I, when the King was a man of pedantic learning who governed by Divine Right, a concept she naturally finds attractive. The universities respond immediately and the dons crowd around her in their academic dress ready to be of service. Their spokesman is the 'Aristarchus' (a classical critic whose name became synonymous with severity) Richard Bentley, the greatest classicist of his day, who had mangled Milton by treating him as a 'dead' text requiring lots of emendation. Bentley is the voice of the pedantic footnotes to *The Dunciad* (some of which bear his name). With his critical microscope he pores over the minutiae of the text-body, but ignores

148

> How parts relate to parts, or they to whole,
> The body's harmony, the beaming soul
>
> (iv, 235–6)

If Bentley has narrowed his world down, then the figure who now enters has done the exact opposite. The young man back from the Grand Tour of Europe (iv, 282) has ranged the continent sampling the vices of the court, the opera-house and the brothel, losing his classical learning and developing expensive and degraded tastes. Both these contrasting characters are in Dulness's grip: Bentley by his dehumanized intellect, the youth by his restless self-indulgence. Dulness claims them both because each fails to express the human within a human scale. One constricts life's energies, the other dissipates them. Thus, however much they seem to represent opposing forces, they embody a single principle. Likewise in each case the master–pupil relationship has gone wrong. The key here is Pope's couplet in *Windsor Forest* expressing the balanced forces of Nature:

> As some coy Nymph her Lover's warm Address
> Nor quite indulges, nor can quite repress.
>
> (19–20)

To *repress* and to *indulge*. In *The Dunciad* both are taken to an extreme: Bentley (by repressing) and the Governor (by indulging) are each working against the principle of nature and its proper growth.

Book Four continues with a lively pageant of figures: the two antiquarian coin-collectors (Annius and Mummius) disputing ownership of a coin that Annius has swallowed – a brilliant image of the age-old connection between muck and brass; the crowd of 'virtuosi' (connoisseurs and collectors of curiosities) which includes two obsessive innocents, the flower-grower and butterfly-collector; the deistical clergyman who believes that reason, not faith, is the path to God, and therefore measures God by the limited capacities of man; and Thomas Gordon ('Silenus'), the translator of the Roman historian Tacitus, who sums up the progress of a youth through the academy of Dulness (iv, 499–516).

Dulness's power is summed up in the '*Cup* of *Self-Love*' (Pope's own note to iv, 517), the symbolic pledge to Dulness which all her devotees drink. Now they are assembled the goddess performs the final ritual of the poem: the conferment of her titles and degrees, where she mimics the King, the University Chancellor and the Worshipful Master. She gives her blessing to the assembled hordes and sends them into the world on their mission to 'MAKE ONE MIGHTY DUNCIAD OF THE

LAND!' (iv, 604). With that, Nature herself begins to nod and the soporific wave of Dulness spreads like some invisible cloud of radiation across the country and over the sea. A line of asterisks ('little stars') across the page signifies a yawning gap, but also hints at the rapidly advancing darkness. But even the stars fade as all human powers and principles are extinguished and the world sinks into 'a total oblivion of all Obligations, divine, civil, moral, or rational' (Pope's *Argument* to Book Four). In the final line of text chaos and eternal night envelop not just the poem, but the poet himself – a mark of commitment to his vision, but also a hint that Pope's own principles will be the last to go.

(iii) The Nature of Dulness

It is impossible to separate the character of the poem from the nature of its generating principle, for that is what Dulness is. The obsessiveness of Dulness is reflected in the obsessiveness of the poem's imagery; the restless changeability of Dulness is present in the fluidity of the poem's techniques. It is fitting that *The Dunciad* should be imprinted with the attributes of the 'Mighty Mother' who broods over it, and the poem's obvious difficulties (especially for a modern reader) may be lessened if we remember that what disturbs, antagonizes or mystifies us in the poem may be Dulness herself.

Pope's goddess Dulness is, after all, very far from dull. In this poem Pope is not attacking the boring, ignorant and lazy (if so, there would be no point in his calling them all to life and involving them in so much frenetic activity). No, as Pope explains in a footnote to i, 15:

Dulness here is not to be taken contractedly for mere Stupidity, but in the enlarged sense of the word, for all Slowness of Apprehension, Shortness of Sight, or imperfect Sense of things. It includes (as we see by the Poet's own words) Labour, Industry, and some degree of Activity and Boldness: a ruling principle not inert, but turning topsy-turvy the Understanding, and inducing an Anarchy or confused State of Mind.

The Dunciad is an extremely active and restless poem. The goddess herself is 'of Bus'ness the directing soul' (i, 169) and is introduced categorically as 'Laborious, heavy, busy, bold, and blind' (i, 15), a line which captures exactly the range of ideas Pope wants to associate with the ruling principle of his poem.

This busy-ness is the first problem that any reader confronts when tackling *The Dunciad*. It is a dense poem, hard to disentangle and difficult to visualize clearly. The impression is created of an enormously fertile imagination running riot, with incidents and characters crowding into the picture from all directions, registering briefly, but being shouldered out of the way as new matter bursts in. The usual care that Pope takes over clear transitions, modulations of tone and the focusing of episodes (evident in such poems as *Windsor Forest* or *Epistle to Arbuthnot*) often seems to have been abandoned. This gives us our first clue as to the nature of the goddess and how she is influencing her poem: we are never given a fixed or consistent image of her. Her first appearance before her worshipper Cibber is typical:

> Her ample presence fills up all the place;
> A veil of fogs dilates her awful face:
> Great in her charms! as when on Shrieves and May'rs
> She looks, and breathes herself into their airs.
>
> (i, 261–4)

She seems at this point to be mere air, a mist which infuses itself into her followers. At another moment (i, 45–54) she stands majestically like the engraved frontispiece to a book, enthroned 'in clouded Majesty' and supported by her 'guardian Virtues'. Shortly afterwards she is 'the cloud-compelling Queen . . . tinsel'd o'er in robes of varying hues' (i, 79–81). She seems to move along with the dunces as the action switches location across London, and all the time there is associated with her a kind of misty, obscured brightness and an ability, like cloud, to dilate and change shape.

The combined imagery of restless movement and shifting cloud runs throughout the poem. For example, as Dulness in Book One watches 'the madness of the mazy dance' she does so 'thro' fogs, that magnify the scene' (i, 68, 80); and when Cibber prays to the goddess to 'spread a healing mist before the mind' (i, 174) he naturally seizes on an image of erratic movement:

> O thou! of Bus'ness the directing soul!
> To this our head like byass to the bowl,
> Which, as more pond'rous, made its aim more true,
> Obliquely wadling to the mark in view
>
> (i, 169–72)

The impression gained is of groping around in the mist, of not having a clear sense of direction. This is central to the concept of Dulness: under her influence there is great expenditure of energy, but it is directionless,

151

undisciplined and shortsighted (we should remember that to be 'dull-sighted' meant to be shortsighted or have some defect of vision). The games in Book Two are full of examples of misdirected energy and erratic movement:

> As when a dab-chick waddles thro' the copse
> On feet and wings, and flies, and wades, and hops;
> So lab'ring on, with shoulders, hands, and head,
> Wide as a wind-mill all his figure spread,
> With arms expanded . . .

> (ii, 63–7)

The awkwardly rushing Curll is heading for a fall. The figure of William Arnall, displaying his skill at mud-diving, makes no progress at all:

> with a weight of skull,
> Furious he dives, precipitately dull.
> Whirlpools and storms his circling arm invest,
> With all the might of gravitation blest.
> No crab more active in the dirty dance,
> Downward to climb, and backward to advance.

> (ii, 315–20)

This moves us on to the associated imagery of gravitation and magnetic attraction. *The Dunciad* is to some extent a poem about gravity. And just as in philosophy writers were searching for the moral equivalent of Newton's principle (to account for human behaviour), so Pope's principle of Dulness is best seen as reminiscent of, but finally in opposition to, Newtonian gravity. Newton's principle sustains order and holds the system of the universe miraculously in place; Dulness's principle drags everything into a vortex (whirlpool) which swirls faster and faster until all collapses into the psychic equivalent of a black hole. The poet James Thomson had praised Newton in 1727 for rescuing the heavens 'from the wide rule/Of whirling vortices' and restoring them 'to their first great simplicity' (*To the Memory of Sir Isaac Newton*, 82–4). Dulness appears to work in exactly the opposite direction, so that she is an anti-Newton, the opposing force to that which Pope celebrated in his famous epitaph:

> Nature, and Nature's Laws lay hid in Night.
> God said, *Let Newton be*! and All was *Light*.

Dulness's command, in contrast, brings eternal darkness.

The progress of Pope's poem towards the extinction of light is a journey around the vortex, and we see many individuals from all walks of life submit in their different ways to the principle of Dulness and allow themselves to be dragged into this imploding system:

> The young, the old, who feel her inward sway,
> One instinct seizes, and transports away.
> None need a guide, by sure Attraction led,
> And strong impulsive gravity of Head:
> None want a place, for all their Centre found,
> Hung to the Goddess, and coher'd around.
> Not closer, orb in orb, conglob'd are seen
> The buzzing Bees about their dusky Queen.
>
> The gath'ring number, as it moves along,
> Involves a vast involuntary throng,
> Who gently drawn, and struggling less and less,
> Roll in her Vortex, and her pow'r confess.
>
> (iv, 73–84)

A key word here is *involuntary*: these figures have surrendered their free will and have become part of a mass movement. In doing so they are belittled, undignified, undifferentiated.

Dulness is not a 'character'. She does not even have an independent existence. She is a driving force within human beings and tends to take the form of their desires, ambitions and obsessions. She is the gleam in their eye, their dream of power, their fantasy, the inner voice that whispers to each individual in terms such as these: *the world is as YOU see it. All your feelings and thoughts are valid, because truth is what YOU (with my help) wish to make it. I will free you from all structures of thought or norms of behaviour, all responsibility to the past, to external judgement or objective standards. Infused with my power ALL is possible. I will inspire you with belief in yourself and the freedom to assert it. I will sanction your language, your ambitions, and your desires.* In succumbing to this tempting voice a person believes he has discovered self-expression; but on the contrary, he has been drawn into the vortex of Dulness, into an enclosed system of selfhood. In asserting the primacy of his own will he has in fact submitted his will to the goddess.

When Cibber is granted a vision of the 'new world to Nature's laws unknown' (iii, 241) he is ecstatic, and there follows an interesting exchange between himself and his father-figure Settle:

> Joy fills his soul, joy innocent of thought;
> 'What pow'r, he cries, what pow'r these wonders wrought?'

153

> 'Son; what thou seek'st is in thee! Look, and find
> Each Monster meets his likeness in thy mind.'

(iii, 249–52)

The keynote here is the notion of 'subjectivity', a tendency to believe
that everything is as we see it and to project our desires, prejudices and
obsessions on to the world around us. Dulness is, therefore, not an
external power, but an inner motivating force, and one that is self-
flattering and self-deceiving:

> Kind Self-conceit to some her glass applies,
> Which no one looks in with another's eyes:
> But as the Flatt'rer or Dependant paint,
> Beholds himself a Patriot, Chief, or Saint.

(iv, 533–6)

In the world of Dulness there are no objective standards, no structures
of ideas against which to measure the truth.

The dunce is freed from structures, and it is significant that there are
no structures in the poem. Instead of stone (out of which containing
structures can be made) there is *lead,* a heavy, dull metal which can be
melted down to take various forms, like the ponderous nonsense which
fills Cibber's skull:

> Nonsense precipitate, like running Lead,
> That slip'd thro' Cracks and Zig-zags of the Head

(i, 123–4)

Or it can be forged into the 'byass' on a bowl (which pulls it out of its
true line), or into heavy bullets or the lead weight in a grandfather clock:

> As, forc'd from wind-guns, lead itself can fly,
> And pond'rous slugs cut swiftly thro the sky;
> As clocks to weight their nimble motion owe,
> The wheels above urg'd by the load below:
> Me Emptiness, and Dulness could inspire

(i, 181–5)

The parody of true inspiration and aspiration is clear. Where genuine
aspiration yearns upwards, movements in *The Dunciad* are either erratic,
circling, or resolutely downwards. Cibber, in searching for inspiration, is
inevitably drawn to the lower reaches of his mind:

> Sinking from thought to thought, a vast profound!
> Plung'd for his sense, but found no bottom there,

> Yet wrote and flounder'd on, in mere despair.
> Round him much Embryo, much Abortion lay,
> Much future Ode, and abdicated Play
>
> (i, 118–22)

And Smedley believes he has had a wondrous vision in the muddy depths of Fleet Ditch.

At moments like these there are strong suggestions of fertility and creativity, and this is appropriate since Dulness is also extraordinarily fertile. Her creations are continuously emerging from the great muddy spawning-ground of Chaos (i, 55–62), but they tend to remain embryos and abortions, strange births from ill-matched parents:

> All that on Folly Frenzy could beget,
> Fruits of dull Heat, and Sooterkins of Wit.
>
> (i, 125–6)

(A *sooterkin* was a small animal, about the size of a mouse, which by popular superstition was born to Dutch women who had the habit of placing stoves under their petticoats.) Dunce-creations are incongruous, piecemeal things which achieve no clear identity of their own:

> A past, vamp'd, future, old, reviv'd, new piece,
> 'Twixt Plautus, Fletcher, Shakespear, and Corneille
>
> (i, 284–5)

Either their identities chop and change, or they merge one into another ('Prologues into Prefaces decay,/And these to Notes are fritter'd quite away', i, 277–8), and this idea of merging becomes a controlling idea in *The Dunciad*.

We have already noted the fluid narrative technique of the poem, and Pope extends this to the theme of the whole. In his hands a large number of contrasting figures (John Rich, Thomas Hearne, Dr Busby, John Curll, the laced governor, Mummius, the sceptical theologian, the operatic diva, the horticulturist – to list only a few) are drawn together and merge into the same movement. Characters who in real life would probably never encounter one another here co-operate in a single enterprise, and for all their quirky individuality they tend to band together as children all serving their goddess-mother.

To say that *The Dunciad* is a paranoid poem is not to dismiss or criticize it, but to locate the source of its power. Pope sets out to convince us that *they are all in it together*, that Dulness insidiously claims each one of us, infiltrating into all professions and classes, and growing in power. But what Pope gives us is not merely a poetic version of a zombie nightmare, but a brilliant analysis of a culture in decay, a society that has lost its sense of responsibility and direction. Nor is it merely 'paranoid' to discern a linking principle in such a hotch-potch of characters. We have already seen how Dulness is a driving force of pride and self-centredness. All the duncers are pursuing some kind of inner vision or obsession; each is craving self-satisfaction and pursuing his own ends. None is concerned to place his actions in a wider context, whether it is John Rich delighting in his fantastic pantomime-world, Booth 'in his cloudy tabernacle shrin'd' (iii, 267), Dr Busby imprisoning the minds of children with his motto 'the narrower is the better' (iv, 152), or the microscopic scientist:

> 'O! would the Sons of Men once think their Eyes
> And Reason giv'n them but to study *Flies?*
> See Nature in some partial narrow shape,
> And let the Author of the Whole escape

(iv, 453–6)

Each is in some way confusing or distorting 'Nature'. Even the young man fresh from the Grand Tour has used his journey across Europe merely to indulge himself rather than widen his perspectives, and in doing so has spent his money and energies to no end ('And last turn'd *Air*', iv, 322). He has thrown away the opportunity to broaden his understanding and deepen his appreciation of European civilization. What Pope values is a culture that will draw nourishment from the past and value shared experience (the common 'currency' of humanity, rather than the hoarded coin of Annius). Pope's positives are those notions dismissed by the 'gloomy clerk':

> Let others creep by timid steps, and slow,
> On plain Experience lay foundations low,
> By common sense to common knowledge bred,
> And last, to Nature's Cause thro' Nature led.

(iv, 465–8)

'Culture' nowadays seems a rather narrow term, and it is perhaps one result of the progress of Dulness that this is so. We must finally remind ourselves that *The Dunciad* is shaped in the epic mould and is a document that demands to be read in terms of a great classical tradition. Perhaps Pope's severest judgement on the duncers is the extent to which they and their activities are travesties of the noble figures and great actions of the past. Pope triumphantly resists the principle of Dulness (however vividly he mimics it) by asserting a tradition and a standard against which the activities of Dulness may be measured. The dunces all fall crudely and lamentably short; they have no dignity, no common sense, no love, no social conscience.

The final point to be made about Dulness, then, is her relationship to this epic world, and the extent to which she reverses its principles. She is formally addressed at the opening with the confidence of Virgil beginning his great *Aeneid*. 'The Mighty Mother, and her Son' could almost be Venus, goddess of beauty, and her mortal son Aeneas, the hero whose adventures Virgil traced from his escape after the destruction of Troy to his founding of what was to be the great empire of Rome and its classical civilization. But the empire that the goddess Dulness and her son are to establish will consume the whole world in darkness. Dulness, 'Daughter of Chaos and eternal Night' (i, 12) is to work outwards from her base among the hack journalists, pamphleteers and publishers of the City of London, to the court and parliament at St James's and Westminster, from the fairs and pageants to the theatres. She will envelop all classes and professions, reaching out to the Oxford scholar in his library, the headmasters of the public schools, the antiquarians and virtuosi, the theologians and the nobility. A pattern begun in the Dark Ages with the migration westwards of the Goths and Huns who sacked the Eternal City, will be repeated in Britain as Dulness's influence spreads, wave upon wave, and eventually extinguishes all learning, arts and religion. This Doomsday Scenario provides the shape of Pope's anti-epic.

All the material of epic is here, but is twisted and distorted in the service of Dulness: epic incidents (the hero's descent into the Shades, heroic games, propitiatory sacrifices, single combats, power struggles, ceremonies, tributes, prophecies, revelations, divine manifestations) are enacted in a kind of black farce, with heroic emotions and attributes turned to grotesque parody: aspiration, pride, courage, faith, constancy, honour – all are acted out before our eyes, but in contexts which recast them as degradation, pomposity, stupidity, madness, obsession and megalomania.

When the Divine Word is finally revealed, it is the '*un*creating word' (iv, 654), the reverse of the creating word (or *logos*) of God. And the empire that finally triumphs is that of Chaos, sire of the goddess Dulness, as though the world, which began in the primordial slime where everything existed only as indistinguishable matter, will in the end return to that state. The Renaissance had looked back to Virgil's epic as celebrating the spread of civilization and enlightenment, and Milton had unfolded the vast providential coherence of history to the marvelling Adam; Pope's *Dunciad*, however, predicts the final days when the whole system will not merely regress to the Dark Ages again, but will implode back into its original matter, as if thousands of years of human history were just a single pulse-beat of a massive impersonal organism.

These are visions which are particularly unsettling to modern man, even more at the end of the twentieth century than in the middle of the eighteenth. Increasingly we are coming to understand how the mad visions of the few, combined with the passive mindlessness of the many, could conceivably bring the end of the world. The prophecies of *The Dunciad* are coming closer to us, and it is becoming easier to discern a relationship between a pacifying mass culture (increasingly international in its spread), the growth of mass movements (political, racial or religious), and the concentration of power in the hands of a few charismatic figures (rock stars, religious figureheads or national leaders). The pseudo-energy of Dulness, with her flagrant appeal to selfish instincts in the guise of freedom, and her neglect of common forms and shared responsibility, is a principle which is still alive, and still threatens us.

14. Suggestions for Further Reading

REFERENCE BOOKS AND EDITIONS

John Butt (gen. ed.), *The Twickenham Edition of the Poems of Alexander Pope*, 11 vols (London and New Haven, 1939–69). This is the standard edition of Pope and is available in an excellent condensed one-volume paperback.

Maynard Mack, *Alexander Pope. A Life* (London and New Haven, 1985). A masterpiece of scholarship and wisdom, and the fruit of a lifetime's study of Pope.

Joseph Spence, *Observations, Anecdotes, and Characters of Books and Men*, ed. James M. Osborn, 2 vols (Oxford, 1966). An invaluable record of Pope's conversation.

J. V. Guerinot, *Pamphlet Attacks on Alexander Pope, 1711–1744: A Descriptive Bibliography* (London, 1969).

George Sherburn (ed.), *The Correspondence of Alexander Pope*, 5 vols (Oxford, 1956).

Paul Hammond (ed.), *Selected Prose of Alexander Pope* (Cambridge, 1987).

John Barnard (ed.), *Pope: The Critical Heritage* (London, 1973). A historical anthology of Pope criticism.

CRITICISM

J. S. Cunningham, *Pope: The Rape of the Lock* (London, 1961).

Peter Dixon, *The World of Pope's Satires* (London, 1968).

T. R. Edwards, *This Dark Estate: A Reading of Pope* (Berkeley, 1963).

Howard Erskine-Hill, *The Social Milieu of Alexander Pope* (New Haven and London, 1975).

Howard Erskine-Hill, *Pope: The Dunciad* (London, 1972).

Howard Erskine-Hill and Anne Smith (eds), *The Art of Alexander Pope* (London, 1979). A collection of critical essays.

David Fairer, *Pope's Imagination* (Manchester, 1984).

Brean S. Hammond, *Pope* (Brighton, 1986).

Maynard Mack, *The Garden and the City: Retirement and Politics in the Later Poetry of Pope, 1731–1743* (Toronto and London, 1969).

Pat Rogers, *An Introduction to Pope* (London, 1975).

John E. Sitter, *The Poetry of Pope's 'Dunciad'* (Minneapolis, 1971).

Patricia M. Spacks, *An Argument of Images: The Poetry of Alexander Pope* (Cambridge, Mass., 1971).

Critical Studies: Poetry of Alexander Pope

Frank Stack, *Pope and Horace: Studies in Imitation* (Cambridge, London and New York, 1985).

Howard D. Weinbrot, *The Formal Strain: Studies in Augustan Imitation and Satire* (Chicago and London, 1969).

Aubrey L. Williams, *Pope's 'Dunciad': A Study of its Meaning* (London, 1955).